EVERY REQUISITE FOR A CAMPAIGN UPON THE GOLD-FIELDS

ORGANISATION, VICTIMISATION AND MYTHMAKING OF
THE WALK FROM ROBE

BY
MICHAEL WILLIAMS

While every precaution has been taken in the preparation of this book, the publisher assumes no responsibility for errors or omissions, or for damages resulting from the use of the information contained herein.

EVERY REQUISITE FOR A CAMPAIGN UPON THE GOLDFIELDS

Second edition. July 30, 2025.

Copyright © 2024 Michael Williams.

ISBN: 978-1763560512

Written by Michael Williams.

Published by ChideStudy Press

For inquires or to order copies email: ChidestudyPress@gmail.com

Website: chidestudypress.com.au

They had a very large number of baskets, with a small proportion of small casks, boxes, cases, and tubs, in which were stowed every requisite for a campaign upon the goldfields.

The Age, 10 April 1855, p.5.

Cover Illustrations:
NLA: Philips' new map of the gold producing colonies of Australia, George Philip & Son, 1853.

Statue in front of Gum San Chinese Heritage Centre, author's photo, April 2022.

Published by: *Chidestudy Press*, 2024
ISBN: 978-1-7635605-1-2

Contents

INTRODUCTION 1

TO STOP THE PROGRESS OF CIVILIZATION WITH A POLL-TAX – BY WAY OF A PREFACE 1

PART I 4

(1) THROWING DOWN A GAGE TO THE CELESTIAL EMPIRE – THE BARE FACTS 4
(2) AN AGE OF CANTONESE DIASPORIC EXPANSION – SOME HISTORICAL CONTEXT 14
(3) AS IF THEY WERE A DETACHMENT OF DISCIPLINED MEN - ORGANISATION 40
(4) A MORE THAN USUAL DEGREE OF ACTIVITY – ARRIVAL AND DEPARTURE 66
(5) BECAUSE THERE WAS NO PENAL CLAUSE – THE OFFICIAL RESPONSE 85
(6) BOATS AT A REASONABLE RATE – WHAT IT ALL COST 95
(7) THE WHOLE ATMOSPHERE WAS CHINESE – HUMPING THE SWAG 110
(8) THE NATIVES RAPIDLY DISAPPEARING – WHOSE LAND? 122
(9) MORE THAN ONCE WAS SEEN TO SHED TEARS - HARDSHIP & SELF-HELP.... 127

PART II 154

(10) WELLS, WALLS AND WOOLSHEDS – FOLKLORE & MYTHS 154
(11) SO, THERE YOU ARE - WHY MYTHS AND WHY THEY PERSIST?................ 232

CONCLUSION 266

(12) WRAPPING UP – PARALLEL HISTORIES & A NEW GENERATION OF MYTHS 266

REFERENCES 270

ACKNOWLEDGEMENTS 279

AUTHOR BIO 282

ENDNOTES 283

INDEX 304

Introduction

To stop the progress of civilization with a poll-tax – by way of a preface

Of the many episodes that make up the oftentimes exotic impression of Chinese Australian history the 1850s walk from the small port of Robe in South Australia to the goldfields of Victoria has repeatedly taken on epic proportions.[1] Its 'long march' like length, tales of hardship and death, not to mention present-day outrage at the discriminatory tax the walk was designed to avoid, all combine to make the stuff of legends. Yet remarkably the telling of this history has largely been left to local historians with their characteristic eagerness to retell every tale and make use of every allusion to their subject with little regard to plausibility, contradiction or even relevance.[2] Thus, while the arrival of thousands of gold seekers from southern China in the mid-1850s at Robe town on Guichen Bay, South Australia, in order to avoid taxes imposed by the neighbouring gold rich colony of Victoria is well known, it is surprisingly little understood in detail.

The bare bones of this history is that, frightened at the numbers of Chinese miners flocking to its goldfields, the

1

new and tiny Colony of Victoria in 1855 imposed a tax on these arrivals as well as a limit to the numbers of Chinese passengers allowed per ship.✦ The most obvious result of these restrictions was a shift in disembarkation point from Port Philip (Melbourne) to at first Port Adelaide and then increasingly to Guichen Bay (Robe), just across the border in South Australia from where many thousands walked many hundreds of kilometres to arrive at the Victorian goldfields. Before South Australia enacted its own similar legislation, some 16,000 Chinese gold seekers had arrived at Robe, most in 1857, and moved on. If the story was left here there would be little for a fastidious historian to complain about.

Unfortunately for the fastidious historian, and presumably for the merely intelligent reader also, this story is invariably embellished with accounts of ill-treatment by unscrupulous ship captains amounting to being thrown overboard in some cases.[3] Overcharging, false guides, and a lack of preparation resulting in numerous deaths along the way (paralleled with such an excess of preparation that handsome limestone wells were apparently dug also), complete the tale. The too ready

---

✦ Tiny – its population of 77,000 in 1851 was still only 200,000 in 1854; new – separation from NSW and self-government was granted in 1850 and a semi-democratic legislature in 1855.

acceptance of this mix of variously sourced tales, myths and actual history are generally the result of a lack of background and context. This is a lack common in Australian history whereby "the Chinese" appear and disappear with little or no regard for where they came from or why. Chinese people are usually seen as a perpetually exotic element condemned in the past, sympathised with or even heroized in the present, but rarely as an intrinsic element of Australian history. It is proposed here therefore to provide some of this necessary background and context along with a detailed retelling of the history of the Robe Walk in order to tease out the remarkable from the mundane. In addition to recounting a history of the walk in terms of motivations and organisation of the Chinese gold seekers, the various myths and tales most commonly associated with this history will be examined along with discussion of their origins, prevalence and persistence, oftentimes in the face of great implausibility and even contradiction.

Part I

(1) Throwing down a gage to the celestial empire – the bare facts

The gold rushes began in the Australian colonies in 1851 with hundreds of thousands of gold seekers arriving, mainly from Europe, in the years immediately following. Chinese gold seekers however didn't begin arriving in numbers until early 1853, although they had already joined the rush to California in the early 1850s.[4] The shift to the Victorian goldfields was not a surprising one given that Hong Kong was the same port of embarkation to any of the "white settler nations" with California and Victoria (Australia) referred to thereafter as the "old" and "new" goldfields (金山) respectively by those from the identical Pearl River Delta districts.♦

♦ The more popular "Gold Mountain" is now the ubiquitous translation for the Chinese characters 金山 (gum san / jin shan) but is in fact a translation choice over the more accurate if prosaic "goldfields". This is a preference that seeks to make exotic what for Europeans was considered normal – namely, rushing to goldfields. While an attractive term that is good for titles of novels and films it should be noted that it continues to play a role in that 'othering' of Chinese people that began in this period. For more on the Pearl River Delta see below.

The Colony of Victoria had only gained a separate existence from the Colony of New South Wales in 1850 and with a tiny population and an inflated sense of destiny it's governing class immediately felt overwhelmed by the arrival of newcomers.[1]♣ While its apprehension of people from China is well known, in fact the first efforts of the Colony of Victoria at stemming the flow of "outsiders" was directed at people from Tasmania (then called Vandemonians).[5] Denied this first attempt at population control by their British overlords, the next effort was directed at "The Chinese Question" and a two-pronged discriminatory restriction was imposed on arrivals of Chinese people that began to come into effect at the end of 1855.

'The leading champion who threw down his gage to the celestial empire was Mr. Fyfe'. Fyfe proposed the tonnage restrictions as a variation on the existing Passenger Acts originally designed to limit overcrowding and associated deaths on ships.[6] This restriction was in addition to a direct

---

♣ As a contemporary poem put it:
> From the gold-tinted sky to the ground, you
> Can see that I'm worthy the Queen.
> In her Majesty's Crown I'm a jewel,
> No brighter one there do you see,
> So, take it (dear Sydney!) not cruel,
> The royal name has been given to me.
>
> *The Argus*, 29 October 1850, p.4.

£10 poll tax to be paid by all Chinese arrivals.[7] The passing of this tax however was not done without opposition citing both practical and moral considerations: 'I cannot but strike with strange again how the Chinese are only taxed and no other kinds of people —have they done anything better than the Chinese?'[8] This opposition included a rare acknowledgement of the hypocrisy of those who 'have wrested from the rightful owner the soil of the country.'[9]

The reaction to this legal change was just as swift as the spread of the news of gold itself as ships captains and agents, both European and Chinese, in Hong Kong and also the Pearl River Delta villages adjusted.[*] These new taxes affected both the agents and organisers who were extending the capital known as "credit-tickets" that enabled most Pearl River Delta villagers to travel at all, and also the ship owners and captains who carried them as passengers under agreements known as charterparties.[10] The first group needed to calculate the £10 poll tax into the overall costs, while the second were now responsible for an additional £10 on any Chinese passengers over the tonnage limit.[11] The result of the combined efforts of these experienced profit seekers, which some commentators had foreseen, was that

---

[*] For discussion of the Pearl River Delta see below, pp.14-15.

by early 1856 many hundreds of Chinese gold seekers were traveling to Port Adelaide and taking the gold escort route that has been established a few years earlier by South Australians heading to and returning from the Victorian goldfields.♣

In fact, many alternative routes were taken in this first year after the new restrictions, including ferries up the Murray River as far as Maiden's Punt (now Moama/Echuca) and walking a mere 100 kms to the goldfields, or transhipping (usually at Port Adelaide, but also at Sydney and even Launceston) to coastal "screw steamers" and heading for Guichen Bay in order to shorten the walk by some 200 kms.[12] Guichen Bay and its port of Robe town was within the Colony of South Australia and therefore poll tax free for Chinese passengers. South Australians however could take the same steamers further along the coast to Portland in Victoria itself from where, as advertisements such as for the *White Swan* announced, it was '110 miles' (175 kilometres) to the Ararat goldfields.[13]

♣ See below for discussion of South Australians walking to the Victoria goldfields, pp.22-25.

STEAM TO MELBOURNE.

CALLING AT PORTLAND to land Goods and Passengers for **ARARAT GOLD DIGGINGS**, 110 miles from Portland.

THE **WHITE SWAN**, is put off till Saturday, 27th inst., at 3 o'lock for the convenience of parties about to proceed to the above Diggings, on which day she will positively sail.

dc   **WM. P. KIRWOOD.**

Image 1: *White Swan* ad, *Adelaide Times*, 25 August 1857, p.1

Although steamers had been operating in the Australian colonies since the 1830s it wasn't until the 1850s that their use rapidly expanded. It was only in 1847 that the arrival of the first steamer from Sydney in Adelaide, the *Juno*, had been much celebrated.[14] While this, like many things, is commonly attributed to the gold rush, in fact the expansion was already well under way. The long running Hunter River Steam Navigation Company based in NSW, for example, was dissolved in 1851 because "the increasing business of the Company rendered an increase of capital necessary" and the Australasian Steam Navigation Company was created in its place.[15] It was also around this time that the screw propeller became standard, replacing the paddle wheel style as the route to and from Port Adelaide became regular.

Apparently, a walking route via the coastal NSW/Victorian border was also investigated: 'It is well known that interested parties are at present collecting information respecting Twofold Bay (aka Boyd Town, Eden), and some of the neighbouring inlets, with a view of landing their Chinese passengers on that side, ...'[16] But while some walked from Sydney or the NSW goldfields there is no evidence of any landings at Twofold Bay, the route from there to the Victorian goldfields being over the Australian Alps. In fact, the movement between the goldfields of Victoria and NSW was evidently quite complex with, for example, in early 1857: 'A strong mob of celestials, accompanied by loaded drays, passed through Albury on Thursday *enroute* for the Ovens. By their appearance and their familiarity with the English language they were evidently old chums and we believe they have come from Braidwood or Rocky River.'[17]

No mention was made of any poll tax to be levied in discussing these various routes because such a tax was only concerned with arrivals into Victoria by 'port'. Although this issue did cause some discussion between the South Australian and Victorian governments in mid-1856 as to whether the Murray River 'ports' should be included.♦ In the interest of intra-colonial harmony, it was an issue that seems to have been left unresolved.[18] Although the use of this route by Chinese gold seekers seems to have ended around the same time.♣

The year 1856 therefore saw many thousands, perhaps 4,300 as estimated by the Governor of South Australia, that had already evaded the Victorian taxes.♥[19] A simple count of Chinese passengers arriving in 1856 gives the higher number of 6,291.[20] However, this number does not allow for those, such as the 40 reported to have remained on the *Launceston* and who continued onto Melbourne.[21] The lesser number being allowed under the tonnage provisions provided the passengers were also willing to pay the poll tax. That nearly 2,000 were willing and able to pay this tax does seem a little

---

♦ The Victorians tried to assert the Murray ports were included and the South Australians denied it. See, *CORRESPONDENCE relative to the conveyance of CHINESE IMMIGRANTS into VICTORIA by steamers,* via *the RIVER MURRAY*. Ordered by the Legislative Council to be printed, May 6th, 1857.

♣ See discussion, pp.74-76 below.

♥ This number is the amount by which the SA Governor reduced the SA population in 1856 when allowing for Chinese departures to the Victorian diggings.

high and the Governor's estimate of those who walked may be a little low. Even if the walkers in 1856 was as high as 5,000 or so this number is dwarfed by the numbers the following year.

At the beginning of 1857 ships much larger than the coastal steamers began arriving from Hong Kong directly at Guichen Bay. This is when the numbers disembarking at the small port of Robe went from hundreds to thousands with, on at least one occasion, 3,000 people present at one time. This was at a time when the small Robe community was described as having a number of new 'excellent stone buildings' and the Robe Hotel. A hotel at which a meeting was held in early 1857 to arrange 'to enclose the burial-ground with a substantial stone wall'. It is also when there was still no 'public place of worship', which the writer felt was 'the disgrace of our little community'. However, Robe Town did enjoy 'the presence for a few days of an excellent German brass band' to help celebrate the Christmas before the new arrivals began directly from Hong Kong.[22]

These high numbers embarking at Robe continued throughout 1857 until South Australia enacted its own poll tax towards the end of that year. It's definition of 'Chinese' included 'any person born of Chinese parents', thus ensuring no claim to being a British Subject was effective.[23] Again, the response to the fresh tax was rapid and by 1858 new Chinese gold seekers were heading for the NSW goldfields where the gold rush was increasing in any case. The Colony of NSW then introduced its own similar restrictions in 1861 while the South Australian restrictions were repealed at the end of that same year.[24] This change however saw only a relatively small number of arrivals in 1862 and 1863, again via Guichen Bay. Finally, in 1865 the Victorians repealed their arrival taxes, as did NSW in 1867. In the period from 1856 to 1863 therefore some 16,000 gold seekers from southern China are reputed to have walked hundreds of kilometres to the Victorian goldfields via South Australia, most, though by no means all, via Robe on Guichen Bay.

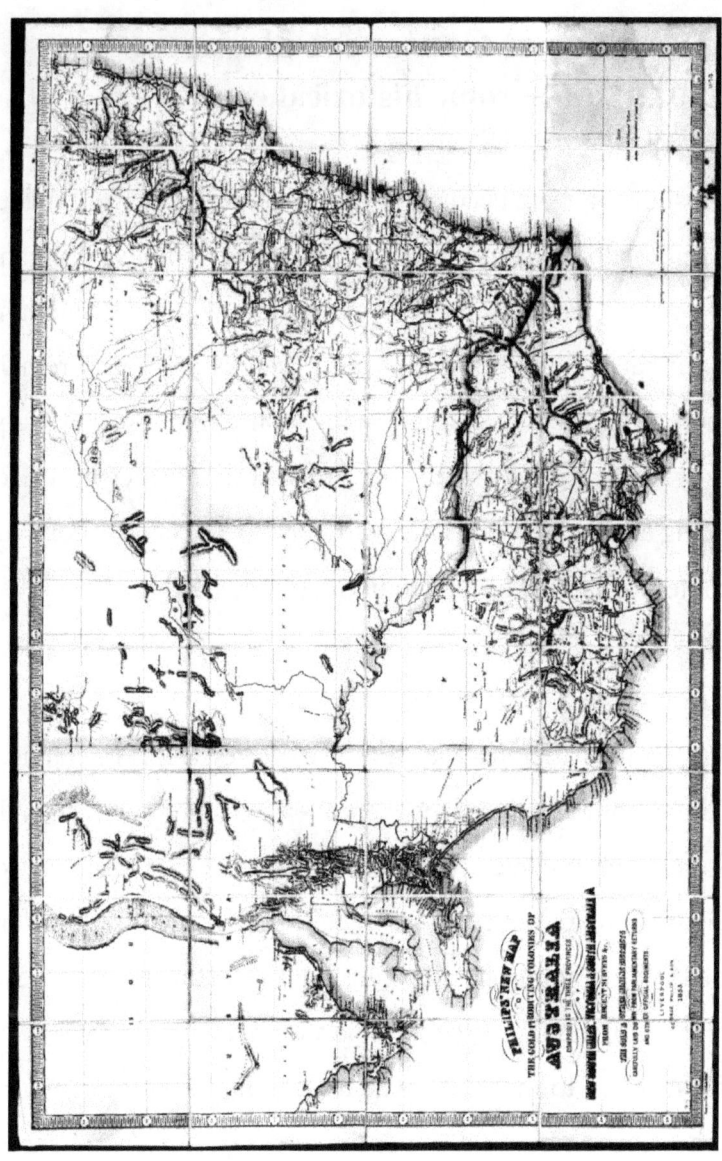

Image 2: Goldfields Map 1852 showing alternative routes from South Australia. NLA: Philips' new map of the gold producing colonies of Australia, George Philip & Son, 1853.

(2) An age of Cantonese diasporic expansion – some historical context

Most of this bare account is well known and in itself makes a remarkable history. However, in history context is all and the wider context here is every bit as remarkable and essential if these "Chinese" gold seekers are not to remain mere long lines of exotic shadows on the landscape. Good only to provide stories of victimisation and racism, or for being assigned responsibility for any infrastructure along the route that is now of uncertain or unknown origin.♦

Pearl River Delta
This context begins with the Pearl River Delta in southern China from which nearly everyone associated with the walk from Robe came. The Pearl River Delta is part of Guangdong province and as such is associated with a history of labour migration stretching back several hundred years and involving the neighbouring province of Guangxi as well as Vietnam to the south. The annexation of Hong Kong by the British in the 1840s after the First Opium War meant for the peoples of the Pearl River Delta counties the advent of an easy connection with European shipping. When

---
♦ See below pp.207-215 for discussion of infrastructure myths.

combined with a tradition of male labour migration this made the Californian and then Victorian gold rushes not only appealing but attainable as far as organisation and financing was concerned. As one scholar of the Late Qing put it, this period can be conceived "as an age of Cantonese diasporic expansion". "… trajectories took Cantonese migrants along the Chinese coast to Shanghai, overland and overseas to Vietnam and elsewhere in Southeast Asia, and overseas to Australasia, the Americas, and Europe."[25]

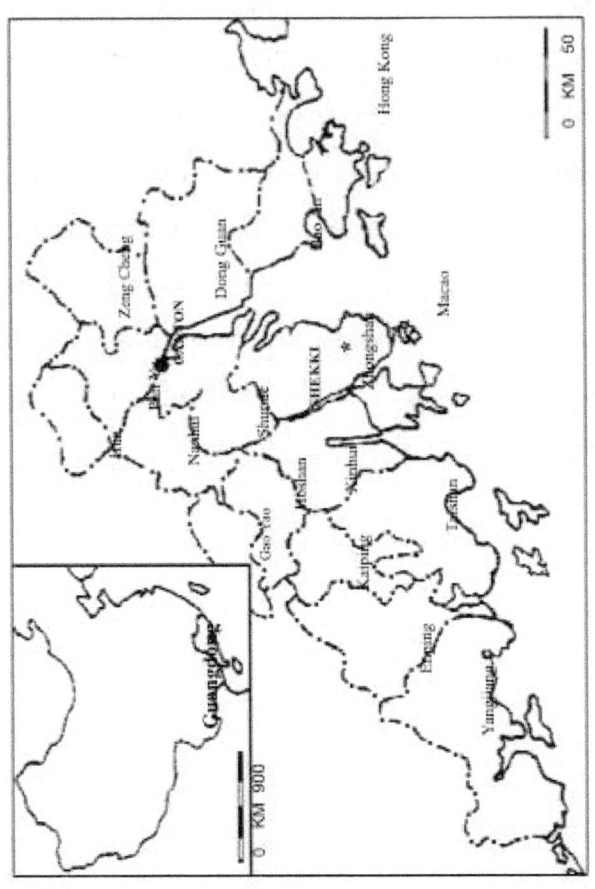

Image 3: Pearl River Delta counties map, from Williams, *Returning Home with Glory*, p.38.

Not the Pearl River Delta?

While the focus here is on arrivals during the gold rush, resident in Victoria and South Australia were a number of pre-goldrush people from the Qing Empire, though not necessarily from the same region as those who later came in search of gold. These included a man named who was robbed of his watch at Gawler in 1845, some men engaged as shepherds coming via Singapore mentioned by the South Australian Governor in 1847, a man named Cossey, one of 'the well-known old identities' of Harrow who died in 1896 but 'who first came to the district in 1851'. The information is sketchy and includes, 'some individuals' who took up work in Adelaide in 1853; 'a Chinaman hutkeeper' who was robbed by bushrangers near Horsham in 1854; as was 'Achee, a Chinese, a shepherd' by 'two natives' in 1855 near Port Lincoln; 'a Chinese carpenter' in the same year whose leg was broken by runaway horse in Adelaide; 'a Chinaman' employed on a station near Horsham in 1856 who witnessed a murder; and on the Murray River route in 1856 there was a 'Chinaman, for some years in the employ of Captain Cadell'.♦[26] Even as late as 1858 three Chinese people are reported as working with sheep at Rocky River, nearly 200 kms north of Adelaide.[27] It is very likely that all these men were from Fujian province and were what are commonly called Amoy indentured labourers.[28] Speaking quite another

---

♦ This last was probably John Egge who later captained his own boats, see Australian Dictionary of Biography.

language they would not have had anything to do with the gold seeking walkers from the Pearl River Delta.

Diversity

Yet while the Pearl River Delta is a relatively small part of China – or more correctly of the then Qing Empire – it is remarkably diverse. Thus, not only did these gold seekers speak a different language from the indentured laborers recruited before the gold rush through Amoy (Xiamen), they also often spoke different languages from each other as well as very distinguishable dialects even within those languages.*[29] This diversity was recognized at the time even by some of the European settlers: 'The men who are now arriving are from the neighborhood of Canton, and are of a different race from those who came last season.'[30] The significance of this diversity and the inadequacy of simply defining everyone as "Chinese" will become obvious as the means of organization, self-identity and self-help that the gold seekers of the Pearl River Delta employed to accomplish their journey is revealed.

---

* The distinction is extremely important even if only because it was important to the Fujian and Cantonese speakers themselves.

The Gold Rush

While understanding the context of the Pearl River Delta gold seekers is important, the gold rushes themselves are also a major context. People from around the world, though mainly from Europe, participated, and both European gold seekers and those from China 'rushed' in similar ways, via sailing ships and then by walking long distances. At the beginning of 1857 a 'SUMMARY FOR ENGLAND' 'for the year 1856' was published for the Colony of Victoria in which it was stated that 125 tons of gold was 'sent away'. This was the gold that had been attracting numerous new arrivals, thus: 'At the commencement of the year 1856 we stated our population at three hundred and twenty-five thousand souls.' Which was 'a nett addition by the seaboard of nineteen thousand four hundred souls.' However, there had been 'no official registration of the movements of the population across the frontiers of the colony to and from New South Wales and South Australia.' So, the increase was no doubt somewhat larger. It is notable that the Chinese gold seekers were counted separately and it was declared that: 'By way of South Australia alone, from ten to twelve thousand of Chinese have reached our gold-fields.'[31]

This figure of 10,000 to 12,000 via South Australia in 1856 would seem to be an exaggeration if the Governor of that colonies own estimate of 4,300 is considered.♦ Nevertheless, it is the perception that was important in determining the reaction to the gold seekers from China. A perception that saw them as distinctly different from European gold seekers. This perception of difference was not of course entirely false. It will be seen that prime differences for those from China was the credit-ticket system, a stronger determination to return home, and being met with a stronger determination to discriminate against them, including of course but not limited to, the poll tax that sparked the diversion via Robe.

Colonialism

The discrimination faced by the gold seekers from the Pearl River Delta was due in part to the colonial context. Among other things this meant British colonies imposing an imitation British society and economy on the recently found to be gold rich landscape at the cost of exterminating the indigenous culture and people if necessary. As observed in South Australia just before the arrival of the gold seekers: 'Large tracts of land are being brought under cultivation.'[32] This meant in South Australia and the neighbouring colonies

---

♦ See above pp.10-11 where perhaps 5,000 was thought possible.

that wool, tree felling, tramways, schemes for river diversion, roads to Melbourne, crown land sales, Land funds, etc, were being actively pursued. All this occurring as the Chinese gold seekers were making their way to the goldfields of the Colony of Victoria. More importantly for this history, it also meant that those with a "British" self-identity generally felt a sense of ownership and entitlement to the land and its resources to the exclusion of even indigenous people and certainly to such non-British people as those who were often declared "Celestials" or subjects of the Emperor of Heaven.

Yet, a feature of British attitudes to their colonies was open immigration. As Richard Graves MacDonald, the Governor of South Australia put it when signing that colonies anti-Chinese immigration restrictions into law in 1861: 'I gave the Queen's assent to that Act … though it evidently contravenes the usual policy of free countries in imposing upon a particular race intending to visit this colony a tax …'[33] This was because British colonialists saw these colonies as profitable enterprises and the more and cheaper labour these had the more profitable they were thought to be. However, this was not the attitude of all of British origin who began to settle in colonies where they were a majority and immigration restrictions began to be imposed, at first temporarily and later permanently.

Contexts – broad and narrow

The broad socioeconomic context within which the Robe Walk took place therefore is threefold. Namely, the labour migration history and practices of the Pearl River Delta; the expanding global colonial enterprise of the Europeans in general and of the British in particular, which encompassed Hong Kong and the Australia colonies; and finally, the global phenomenon that drew them together, the gold rushes. Within these broad contexts, it is also necessary to take note of what might consider fairly obvious contexts, such as the need to walk everywhere, as well as considerations of motivation, racism, indigenous expropriation and travel arrangements.

Walking

Perhaps the most obvious context is that of walking. Writers often refer to the trek of the Chinese gold seekers as a remarkable feat yet it needs be remembered in our era of cars and rapid mechanical transport that walking in large groups to the goldfields was the standard method of operation in the 1850s. From Adelaide alone the 'number of persons, horses, and carts, daily crossing the ferry' in 1852 was reported as 'truly astonishing'.[34] This ferry being one crossing the Murray River at Wellington with that route 'being the direct high-road overland to Melbourne.'[35] As one traveller – himself on a horse – observed enroute from Adelaide to the goldfields in 1852, 'many were on foot, advancing with a firm step, and head erect'.[36] A diary account of the overland route to Mount Alexander in January 1852 refers to often being passed by others, including the 'overland mail man'.[37] Walking is simply how a great many, Chinese or not, got to all the goldfields of Victoria, NSW or Queensland. Just as they also did so when walking via Adelaide and Guichen Bay, with one local asserting that: 'As there are so many hundreds of persons in the colony who have gone overland to the diggings by this route, and are, therefore, intimately acquainted with the locality, it is superfluous to enter into a discussion as to its capabilities."[38] Not all were perhaps so intimately acquainted and for those of us would have been:

> Maps of the Overland Route. — Mr. Platts has now on sale some Maps which will be found exceedingly useful to persons intending to make the overland route to the Diggings. These Maps show the routes hitherto pursued, and also the road opened by Capt. Tolmer in his late successful journey, including the separate stages of each

day's journey, and the localities where water can be procured. The accuracy of the Maps has been confirmed by Capt. Tolmer himself. They are neatly drawn by an experienced draughtsman, and the price is very moderate.[39]

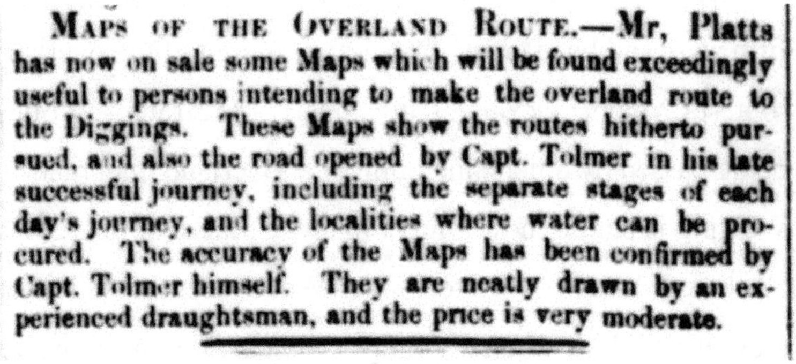

> MAPS OF THE OVERLAND ROUTE.—Mr. Platts has now on sale some Maps which will be found exceedingly useful to persons intending to make the overland route to the Diggings. These Maps show the routes hitherto pursued, and also the road opened by Capt. Tolmer in his late successful journey, including the separate stages of each day's journey, and the localities where water can be procured. The accuracy of the Maps has been confirmed by Capt. Tolmer himself. They are neatly drawn by an experienced draughtsman, and the price is very moderate.

Image 4: Maps ad, *South Australian Register*, 26 March 1852, p.3.

Those walking the overland routes to the goldfields included of course the same route that many Chinese gold seekers would later take and 'since the month of December last [1852], 4000 persons have passed through the Mosquito Plains [Naracoorte] on their way from South Australia to the Mount Alexander diggings.'[40] This was therefore by no means a lonely walk, as when John Broadbent took this route that same year, for example, he met numerous people travelling back from the goldfield and at one point 'there were eight carts, one dray, 16 horses, 12 bullocks, and between 20 and 30 men helping each other through a bog.'[41]

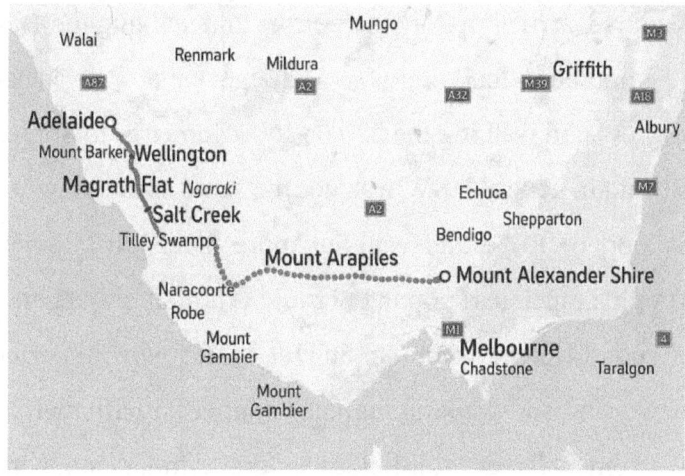

Image 5: Broadbent route

While these accounts of South Australian's making their way to the goldfields date from the early period of the goldrush, it was not the case of the route being left to Chinese gold seekers only a few years later. In 1857, at the peak of the Chinese walkers coming from South Australia, it was noted that many of the new arrivals on the 'Canton Lead, Mount Ararat' (reputedly found by Chinese walkers) also included many 'from South Australia'.[42] Walking would remain common for many years to come and it was only in March 1856, just when the first walkers from the Pearl River Delta were heading off from Adelaide to the goldfields, that the first Adelaide to the port railway journey occurred – with some trepidation.[43]

Of course, arrival in Port Melbourne and walking the 100 to 160 kilometres to Ballarat or Bendigo, or at Port Jackson (Sydney) and walking the 220 or 260 kilometres to Sofala or Hill End in central NSW was not the same as arriving in the tiny port of Robe and walking more than 400 kilometres through a much less populated route. Though it was perhaps not too different from landing at Cooktown in northern Queensland and walking a much rougher 250 kilometres to the Palmer River goldfields as did similar numbers a generation later.[44] Nevertheless, all these walks were done by a great many gold seekers from such places as Britain, Germany, and Chile as well as those from China.

What then was different about the Chinese gold seekers? Certainly, their tendency to arrive in large – 150 to 600 men – well organised groups was one: 'Our correspondent at Langhorne's Creek informs us that about 100 Chinese passed on Friday the 29th, on their overland journey to the diggings, also that eighty-four went by a week before.'[45] This, plus their different clothing and language, styles of eating and sales of knickknacks, all made sure their passing, at Robe or elsewhere, was well noted.[46] Not that those from China did not quickly adapt to their new environment and 'a long string of new-chum Chinamen passed through Linton, some of whom appeared to be exceedingly amused at seeing their fellow countrymen dressed in clothes of European manufacture.'[47]

Image 6: 1854 drawing of Chinese walkers, Charles Lyall, 1854, State Library Victoria H87.63/2/4

Motivation

Yet while differences certainly existed, one in which the Chinese gold seekers perhaps did not differ as much as stereotypes maintain was in their motivation in coming to Australia at all. For many the stereotype and for others the self-serving prejudice, is that the prime motivation of those from the Pearl River Delta was a chaotic fleeing of poverty or war, or even due to a species of enslavement. Superficial non-explanations such as the Taiping Rebellion are rolled out despite the main devastation of that uprising taking place in numerous provinces that sent not a single person to the goldfields of the Pacific.♦[48] The tradition of labour migration of the Pearl River Delta peoples or their closeness to the newly established port of Hong Kong are not even considered in accounts assuming more exotic explanations.

It would appear that while thousands of Europeans simply decided to travel in the hope of finding gold with no more motivation than a hope to better themselves, Chinese gold seekers needed to be pushed by more extreme motivations. While this perspective may be partly based on an awareness of greater devotion to family and village among Chinese than European gold seekers, it is also just as likely to be founded on a sense that 'these people don't belong here'. That is, that as 'coolies' or even slaves 'they' are unfair competition for gold or wages. This last is a trope that

---

♦ Such assumptions are most common in general accounts presented by institutions; unfortunately, these superficial histories are often all many people see.

developed overtime and which in turn fed back to inform many histories of the Chinese in Australia.*⁴⁹

To fully understand the motivations of the Robe walkers it is necessary to be aware of the long history of labour migration by male family members that was part of the Guangfu region (Guangdong and Guangxi provinces) of which the Pearl River Delta was a part. Such members would work in distant locations, remit money to support the family in the village, and return periodically to where parents, wife and children were located. As a rare Chinese goldminer's voice expressed it: 'we wish to leave some of the family to look after our aged parents,' for as 'soon as we get a little money we will try to get home to our aged parents, for our ancient books teach that we must look after our parents.'⁵⁰

Travel on credit

This labour migration was seen as a long-term family investment and was often financed by credit or more specifically by a so-called 'credit-ticket', meaning the trip was financed by agents who were to be repaid from future earnings. This had long been the style for Chinese labour

---

* This basis for many myths is discussed below, Chapter 11.

migration such as reported 20 years before the gold rush in 1831:

> Although the passage-money in a, Chinese junk from Canton to Singapore is but six Spanish dollars, and from Fokein but nine, yet it is commonly paid from the fruits of the emigrant's labour after his arrival, and very rarely in advance.[51]

The gold-rushes saw these methods used to greatly expand the numbers travelling and to organise the movement from village to the trans-Pacific gold fields. This often meant that comparatively younger family members would be sent as a long-term investment with their marriages to be arranged on successful return: 'Among them we noticed many apparently old men, and young boys, and all are of a strong Mongolian cast of features.'[52] Also: 'Among them was a number of young lads, apparently of a livelier temperament than that usually presented by Chinamen on the gold fields.'[53]

This agent-controlled credit-based organisation implies of course that not all who arrived were intending to find their gold by digging for it. Many were agents, traders, or merchants such as when the *Emma* arrived in 1856 with 'a very valuable cargo, shipped by and consigned to Chinese.'[54]

In fact, such merchants travelled as cabin class passengers, as opposed to steerage, and were therefore listed by name.♦[55] Even among those who were intending to dig not all were first timers with this account reputedly written by or in co-operation with a prominent Melbourne based merchant giving a good idea of the back-and-forth nature of the link with Australia as well as the nature of the credit and those who provided it, at least some of the time:

> John has returned to his native village, he has purchased himself a wife, and passed a pleasant honeymoon. But he has by these means got through a good deal of his savings. The local mandarin or some of the sharks from his Yaman begin to "squeeze" his purse rather hard, and though John does not "seem to see it, he must submit, and knows if he continues there he must also continue to submit. Interest and inclination both point to another voyage as the remedy. He either invests the remainder of his money in goods which he forthwith ships for our market, or he pays the passage of some five or six labourers, who will work for him for a certain time subsequent to

---

♦ 'Yung-Chung-Ahoy, Wang-a-Sung, Teng-a-Kong, Tung-a-Pung, Tung-a Yung, Kong-a-Sung, Kong-a-Mee, Chun-a-Chee, Wim-a Sew, Loo-a-Ohang, Kong-a-Lung, and Wat-a-Chan, in the cabin; and 210 other Chinese in the steerage.'

their arrival here. These he will see smuggled in without any poll tax, no matter whether by Guichen Bay or Twofold Bay.* He himself, being able to pay, comes direct to Melbourne, travels inland by Cobb or Clarke, and before the arrival of his labourers has selected the field for their operations, or the situation best fitted for the disposal of his goods.[56]

In a very similar account:

When a Chinaman has been successful, and returns to his own country, he very frequent does not rest satisfied. Many of them invest a portion of their wealth in merchandise suitable for this market, and return with it. Others engage suitable men work for them at the gold-fields, send them to Guichen Bay, but come themselves straight to Melbourne, pay their £10 head-money, go by coach to the goldfields, and search for a locality on which to place their gang of laborers when they come overland. The author knows men who have paid the £10 head-money three times during the short period in which it has been levied.[57]

---

* On the reference to 'Twofold Bay' see p.9 above.

Hong Kong

There is little in all this to indicate that the motivations of gold seekers from the Pearl River Delta were fundamentally different from gold seekers of Dublin, Berlin or London. A general poverty, or at least the desire to gain more wealth, was undoubtedly a common factor but there is no evidence of any especial degree of poverty or famine in the Pearl River Delta during this period. Still less of flight from war, famine or other extraordinary circumstances. It is the relatively narrow distribution of villages and districts that participated in the gold rushes that tells us that proximity to Hong Kong was the prime factor. This, combined with an established history of labour migration, including access to agents and merchants able to provide the initial capital for passage money and equipment, removes the need to imagine famines or rebellions that would make these gold seekers into 'coolies.' The correspondence of districts represented in California, Victoria, NSW, British Columbia and Queensland (though not the proportions) would confirm the port of Hong Kong as the common factor.[58]

None of this is remarkable given the history of Guangdong (廣東) province as its capital Guangzhou (廣州, aka Canton) had long been a major trading port with good river links to the west (Guangxi, 廣西) and sea links out from the Pearl River Delta along the coast to both north and south. When the Qing Empire was still able to resist the demands of European traders, the Portuguese took up a restricted residence in Macao, which was part of the Pearl River Delta County of Hsiangshan, 香山 (aka Zhongshan, 中山), a prominent source of people going to Australia. When the British set up on Hong Kong Island in 1841 and waged two Opium Wars from this base, their warships sailed to Canton along the northern coast of the Pearl River Delta to do so.♦

In fact, it is interesting to note that the flow of gold seekers back and forth through Hong Kong to California and Victoria was apparently unaffected by the Second Opium War (aka Arrow War), which included the shelling of Canton and its brief occupation by British troops.[59] As this "war" was going on, thousands of villagers living just to the south of the fighting were freely travelling to the goldfields and back via the British controlled Hong Kong. This was noted by some but not many in the Australian colonies: 'While England is actually at war with China, immigrants from that country are flocking to our shores.'[60] One South

---

♦ First Opium War 1839–42, Second Opium War 1856–60.

Australian newspaper even discussing the news of British attacks on Canton in which ships 'sent ashore parties of men armed with torches and fire-boxes, with orders to burn and destroy everything within their reach' in one column, while in the next column is news of 'as many as eight vessels are known to be loading at Chinese ports for Port Robe'.[61]

Thus, people of the Pearl River Delta villages had a history of labour migration that found a mass outlet when a foreign colony was created nearby that gave them access to further foreign colonies around the Pacific. A key factor was that just as those Chinese who took up residence on the island of Hong Kong found themselves treated as second-class citizens by its British rulers and merchants, so too did their fellows find similar attitudes prevailing in the white-settler colonies of the Pacific, both British controlled or not, as in the case of California.

Discrimination and racism

The large numbers of people from China travelling to the British colonies of Australia found themselves in the midst of a highly prejudiced and narrow-minded society. Victorians hated Vandemonians, English hated Scots and Irish, British hated Europeans, colonial born hated new arrivals, and everyone hated Indigenous Australians. Class divisions, including contempt for ex-convicts, was widespread, as was the idea that the Christian civilisation they espoused was superior to all others. People of Chinese origin were looked upon as curiosities at best and with contempt after the slightest provocation, if any at all. This was a change noted at the time: 'Some time ago Chinese immigrants, ... appeared to be regarded merely with curiosity. Now, however, the comments of the bystanders are assuming a decidedly unfriendly character.'[62]

This unfriendliness included, in Victoria at least, the establishment of a special official known as the Chinese Protector whose services Chinese people themselves were expected to pay for through a system apparently named without irony 'protection' fees.♦ That the Chinese gold seekers had little respect for such imposts is not unreasonable, although one such protector perhaps thought they should when he reported: 'That the Chinese are in the habit when about to leave the colony, of transferring their Miners Rights and Protection Tickets to others of their

---

♦ No such special official was thought necessary in NSW where Gold Commissioners served a similar function for all miners and were paid from general revenue.

countrymen and as it is impossible to render their names in English, it is equally so to convict them of a wilful fraud."[63]

Indigenous expropriation

One of the most significant contexts and a powerful reason for the fear and rejection of Chinese arrivals in any numbers was of course the intense awareness of the white Europeans that the land they were busy digging gold from had only very recently been expropriated from another people. The land around Guichen Bay for example, through which so many Chinese gold seekers would pass belonged to the Bungandidj people. In the years just prior to the Chinese arrivals, disease, massacres and land expropriation had greatly reduced the numbers of the people of the Bungandidj. Those members of the Bungandidj that had survived lived a semi-traditional lifestyle that included working for the various settlers on occasion and selling food to those travelling through.[64]

Political immaturity

The gold rush itself brought huge population increases into a colony (Victoria) with a governmental structure that was relatively immature. A divergence between the ability to pass laws and the ability to enforce those laws was just one environment in which all gold seekers – Chinese or not –

found themselves. Social unrest was also prevalent with the so-called Eureka Rebellion of 1854 marking a high point in contrast with the Colony of NSW with its more mature administration. All three colonies most concerned had only just been granted a degree of democratic government when the vote was given to all males over 21 years of age. This occurring first in 1856 in South Australia, in 1857 in Victoria, and in 1858 in NSW.

Contextual Summary

The Chinese gold seekers arriving in the Australian colonies were able to do so as a result of European colonisation in both southern China with most notably the establishment of control over Hong Kong as a port, and the recent expropriation of the indigenous peoples of the Australian continent and the legal and social infrastructure that had been established. This meant these southern Chinese villagers were able to take passage, trade and of course export the gold they obtained. At the same time, they entered a social environment in flux and with a great deal of prejudice and narrow mindedness in play. A combination of recent expropriation, an immature government, a nervous sense of identity, sudden population increases, recent voting rights all combined to subject the Chinese gold seekers to a discriminatory environment, one that was often very hostile. Nevertheless, this environment allowed thousands to travel, prosper and return home, often numerous times, and thus to succeed on their own terms.

(3) As if they were a detachment of disciplined men - organisation

Aspects of the organisation of the gold seekers in getting themselves from their villages to the goldfields and back have been touched upon as part of the discussion of the broader context. However, there is much more about the organisation of travel of significance. Before Chinese gold seekers could find themselves in the recently independent colony of Victoria or the older colony of NSW, they had to organise their departure from their villages in southern China. The prime means of doing so for those with limited resources was the credit-ticket system.♦ And it is the credit-ticket system that is one of the prime differences between Chinese and European gold seekers. This is because this method entailed more than simply borrowing money to be repaid in some form. While individual cases varied, the credit-ticket system also involved China or Hong Kong based agents providing not only the finance but just as importantly the organisation to move thousands of villagers through to Hong Kong, onto shipping and then off to distant goldfields. This organisation included, when necessary, taking into account legal changes, as well as providing

---

♦ See pp.29-30 above.

supplies and sufficient oversight to ensure success on the goldfields and therefore a return on the investment.

Indications of organisation

The level of organisation involved can be clearly seen in the large numbers that were successfully brought to the goldfields. Not as people who were desperately poor and constrained to work under any conditions but: 'They seemed to possess a large quantity of stores of one kind or other, to judge from the number of baskets and bundles in their possession' and 'the whole body appeared as comfortable and orderly as if they were a detachment of disciplined men'.[65] Some of these bundles contained goods brought with the specific intention of selling to the locals in exchange for ready cash and 'as soon as they had effected a landing on the wharf, began to sell various articles to those who evinced a desire for the novelties, which comprised curious fans, straw hats, with conical crowns and broad brims, beaded purses, &c.'[66] However, the most obvious indication of the level of organisation was also the one most commented on in the diggings themselves. This was that the Chinese miners tended to work in large groups co-operatively, often with a 'headman', in strong contrast to miners from Europe.♣

Variations

The reach and flexibility of this credit-ticket system is particularly evident when it was faced with distant legal changes and the need to switch routes, meet the requirements of specific disasters, or deal with attempts at fraud. Two things need to be mentioned to qualify this account before proceeding. The first is that any organisation can fail and this undoubtedly did happen on occasion, and secondly that by no means all people coming from the Pearl River Delta would have done so under the most organised version of the credit-ticket system seen here. Others, especially as time when by, undoubtedly travelled as individuals or in smaller groups using either their own money or advances on other terms. The proportion of people that may have travelled on these varying terms it is not possible to say with any certainty.

♣ 'Headman' is the term used in English but was likely a representative of those who advanced the credit if not the one who advanced the credit himself. See, pp.29-30 above.

Response to the news

What was the reaction in Hong Kong and the villages of the Pearl River Delta to news of a new tax enacted by the Colony of Victoria? As discussed above, thousands of these villagers had already travelled to the goldfields of Californian and Victoria and back again, even as the Taiping, Red Turban rebels and the British were taking their turns at disrupting life in their province of origin.[67] The reaction, even at this particularly disrupted point in the Pearl River Delta's history, reveals much about the high degree of organisation as well as about the motivations of those involved.

The Victorian legislators might not have been overly familiar with conditions in the Pearl River Delta, but they were thoroughly familiar with shipping and their trade routes with Hong Kong. Thus while the new law was formally passed by the Victorian Legislative Council in mid-1855, its tax was 'not enforced for at least four months, as otherwise injustice might be done to the charterers of ships from China.'[68] When the *Malacca*, which departed Hong Kong before the new laws could have been known, was reported in September to be bound for Adelaide with 300 Chinese passengers this did not excite any special comment, and when in fact it passed on to Melbourne their arrival in early October seems to have occurred without incident.[69]

The *Malacca* would have perhaps left Hong Kong in July. When news of the new Victorian taxes did reach Hong Kong is not certain, but around early September 1855 is likely. This estimate is based on backdating from the arrival of a Hong Kong report dated late November in which the scheme to land people at Port Adelaide and that 'the trade of Adelaide will be much increased' are commented on.[70] The ship this letter arrived on was the *Launceston* and the embarkation in January 1856 of most of its '310 Chinese passengers' at Port Adelaide with only 40-odd who 'paid their passages to Victoria', would appear to be the first, certainly the first large scale, effort to side-step the Victorian tax.[71] Thus, in the at most three months since Hong Kong and the villages of the Pearl River Delta received the news of the changed circumstances, a planned response had been successfully put in place.

Despite this relatively quick response the Victorians seem to have been at first satisfied that a 'check' had been made in the numbers arriving in the colony. Census numbers reported in the Parliament were that in '1855 the number of arrivals had been 11,403'. And further that: 'When the Chinese Immigrant Act came into operation, a very remarkable check was apparent in the influx, in 1856, the number was reduced to 7325, showing clearly that the provisions of that act had operated in the way intended.'[72] These were the official figures anyway, for as early as February 1856 W.H. Foster, who held the position of 'Chinese Protector' at Ballarat, noted in his diary: 'I am informed that considerable numbers of Chinese are daily arriving on the goldfields coming overland from Adelaide, and thus avoiding the provisions of … the Act. I am told that no less than three hundred are at the present time on the road from Adelaide to this Gold Field.'[73]

Equipped
This response by the Chinese gold seekers did not stop at merely dropping people off at Port Adelaide and leaving them to find their own way to the Victorian goldfields. Those so embarked several hundred kilometres further away than usual came equipped with money and goods to obtain more money and 'as soon as they had effected a landing on the wharf, began to sell various articles to those who evinced a desire for the novelties, which comprised curious fans, straw hats, with conical crowns and broad brims, beaded purses,

&c.'[74] The market completed, they then moved off to their 'Canvas Town'; this or a later site was on Currie Street in the middle of Adelaide, though another site to the east at Kent Town was also used.[75] Not all goods were sold immediately and some carried such items with them. Edward Hearne, working just across the border from South Australia in Victoria stated that: 'Many of these Chinese had with them fancy goods, ornaments, baskets, etc., some of which were bought at the station.'♦[76]

♦ While nothing was said at Adelaide or along the route to Victoria it was reported in Tasmania that 'disgustingly offensive prints and paintings' were also among the items for sale carried and presumably purchased by some locals.

Image 7: Gold seeker's box carried as far as Victoria, private collection.

In addition to selling items, some later arrivals attempted to take up work as 'lumpers' around the port of Adelaide to earn extra cash. However, this angered those who usually undertook such work as 'the low rate of remuneration at which some of the Chinese have lately been employed' threatened their own wages. Foreshadowing later anti-Chinese efforts the result was that 'every means short of those which were punishable by law' were used 'to render the position of the Chinese as unpleasant as possible.'[77]

Routes

From the first, the option of taking a coastal steamer from Port Adelaide to Guichen Bay (Robe town) and thus shorting the walking distance was employed. Thus throughout 1856 the *Burra Burra* made the regular coastal run between Adelaide and Melbourne including taking Chinese gold seekers to Guichen Bay. To Guichen Bay in the relatively small steamers the numbers were in the hundreds, with even smaller numbers continuing to Melbourne. In January 1856, for example, '30 Chinamen, in the steerage' [one for every 10 tons] left for Melbourne on the coastal steamer *Burra Burra*.[78] Those who continued on to Port Philip and paid the £10 poll tax were presumably agents, store owners or perhaps returning diggers with capital who would meet the walkers on the goldfields after taking the coach from Melbourne.

Planning

Exactly how all this was organised between the Pearl River Delta villages – Hong Kong – the ships – Adelaide – Melbourne – and finally the goldfields themselves is not clear. How much was pre-planned and how much determined on the spot for example? There is a report of a small group of just nine Chinese people arriving at Port Adelaide at the beginning of October 1855.[79] Were they perhaps an advance party sent to arrange supplies and contacts for larger groups to follow? Were they the same nine who then took the steamer *Havilah* onto Melbourne in mid-October?♦[80] Adelaide was not an entirely unknown factor in any case as the Singapore – Batavia – West Australia – Adelaide route to Melbourne was common. Additionally, we are told of at least one Chinese person who had made a 'considerable sum' in South Australia before these arrivals.[81] Was it he or another who had earlier arrived by the schooner *Skyrocket* from Guichen Bay in late 1853?[82]

First walkers

♦ The *Havilah* (meaning 'Land of Gold') was the first steamer built for the Port Adelaide to Melbourne route.

49

While many smaller groups (necessarily smaller to be within the one person per 10 tons of ship limit), travelled - including a group of 11 from Melbourne to Adelaide - it was naturally the larger groups that attracted attention.[83] Thus referring to the group that arrived in January 1856 it was felt that 'they will easily make their way overland to Melbourne' (thousands of South Australian residents having already done so).♦[84] The same newspaper had reported that the summer was 'one of the coolest known for many years', which undoubtedly would have helped.[85] This prediction of an easy walk was proven correct when the first arrivals overland from Adelaide arrived in March 1856 on the Victorian goldfields and 'far from suffering incredible hardships, have arrived in rather good condition than otherwise.'[86]

That arrival in 'good condition than otherwise' was achieved is testament to a high level of organisation. This is a standard of organisation we would normally have to postulate, as smooth operations usually inspire little comment.

♦ The *South Australian Register*, published a day-by-day account of a walk to the Mount Alexander diggings in 1852 that took nearly a month.

Fortunately for the historian there are two instances when a breakdown gave rise to discussion of the organisational details. The first was when monies set aside for supplies on the journey were stolen, and the other was when a ship's Captain apparently broke his contractual arrangements with the Hong Kong merchant who chartered his ship.

The first opportunity to peer into the workings of how thousands of Chinese villagers were successfully moved to the Australian goldfields – and this is usually very much a 'peering in' as reliance is overwhelmingly on European observers – occurred at Glen Osmond. This location, now an Adelaide suburb, would at that time have been just outside Adelaide proper at the beginning of the steep climb over the Adelaide Hills. The opportunity to learn how things were organised begins with what was described as 'a heartless robbery' apparently 'perpetrated by one of a party of Chinese' on its 'treasurer'. Though this was disputed and the treasurer himself was suspect and subject to much hostility (included an attempt on his life stopped only by the intervention of 'mounted troopers' and some bloodshed). From the account we learn that not only did the group of 120 men have a sum of money entrusted to a treasurer but they had already bought cattle to take on their journey. The loss of the money, presumably needed to buy provisions on the way, meant a choice to either push on and risk running short, or to sell the cattle and regroup in Adelaide with less meaty but sufficient supplies.[87]

It was decided to par down the groups equipment by selling its 'horses, bullocks, and drays'. A Mr Fitzpatrick, the owner of the land where they were camping – Mountain Hut – was willing to purchase all this 'for £200 cash'. Complicating matters, all this gear came associated with guides who had been 'engaged at £2 per week and their rations for eight weeks certain'. The guides, fearing they would get nothing after three weeks work, wished to claim the bullocks as security. Fitzpatrick, while willing to hold up his sale until the guides were dealt with, also saw the bullocks as security on the '£12 16s. for food supplied to men and beasts'.[88]

Up to the point of being robbed, it can be seen that the group of 120 gold seekers from the Pearl River Delta had done well but now found themselves in a tangle of contractual and debt obligations, not to mention language and no doubt cultural differences. Two men are named as heads of the group – Tacoan and Hungka – and a third as their interpreter – Aligali. These negotiated with the guides and the landowner, with both offering to accept part only of what they felt they were owed. While willing to accept the offer of Fitzpatrick, the claim of the guides was rejected on the grounds that their money was owned to them by 'Patoo, the Chinese guide and treasurer', who was 'well known as a cabinetmaker, residing in Currie-street, and who was engaged to proceed with this body of his countrymen to the diggings' and, it was believed, still had the money.[89] After much back and forth, threats of legal action, and many counter-offers, the guides eventually got £6 each and a chosen party headed to 'Adelaide laden with bank-notes to make ready for a fresh departure'. The plan being to purchase a 'light vehicle' to carry injured members and to look after their own money. It is not known what happened to Patoo the Adelaide cabinetmaker and would be treasurer.[90]

Thus, this early party on the route from Adelaide to the Victorian diggings can be seen to have been sufficiently equipped with capital and organisational ability to survive a large blow and continue on. They had purchased cattle and drays to help transport them and provide food, they had hired guides to assist them and had a connection with Patoo, a man from China already resident in Adelaide. Their well organised and seemingly well financed plans coming undone it would appear only when apparently either Patoo or another proved untrustworthy. Other, presumably similarly well organised groups that did not incur such difficulties and for that reason were less reported on, no doubt also made the journey.

Another group to suffer a mishap and so provide us with more logistical details did so even earlier in its journey to the goldfields and the resulting legal dispute provides insight into the organisation of the trip as far back as Hong Kong. A court case was the result of a Hong Kong based merchant named Ayun suing Edward Josiah Sage, supercargo of the ship *Emma* for falsely claiming money from goods sent on the *Emma* as security. The claim was declared false in part because Sage and the ship's captain, Gill, had only taken the 260 Chinese passengers to Adelaide when they, and the charterer of the ship the Hong Kong based merchant Ayun, had paid with the expectation they would be going to Port Phillip.[91]

As a result of this dispute, we learn that the passengers had each paid (or had had paid for them) from $75 to $90

Mexican dollars.◆ The English-speaking Ayun, who was based in Hong Kong and was a partner in the firm Fong Foo (aka Tong Foo), had signed a 'charterparty' with Edward M'Cormick, the owner of the brig *Emma* of some 260 tons and under a Hawaiian flag, to take passengers to Port Phillip. For this M'Cormick was paid $13,500 – an upfront amount of $10,000 and the balance on arrival - for which some 200 tons of goods, also carried by the *Emma* and to be sold in Victoria, would be security. Ayun and the two 'compradors' would 'provide wood and provisions, water, baths[?], and all requisites for passengers according to law' and see to its distribution. An additional '300 sovereigns' was also provided to meet other expenses.[92]

If the ship had proceeded to Port Phillip as the charter stipulated all would have been straightforward. Instead, much to the annoyance and concern of the Chinese parties, Captain Gill and E. J. Sage went first to Adelaide in mid-April 1856 where they chartered the steamer *Young Australia* at 50 shillings (over £4) per person and along with 15 days provisions sent most of the passengers to Guichen

---

◆ Mexican trade dollars were silver coins used in China and Hong Kong at this time. Around $4Mex were equal to £1 of the British pounds being used in the Australian colonies.

Bay. The consequent walks according to one of Ayun's men who accompanied them, Fong Ah Mun, was in fact 35 days. Hardship nearing 'starvation' was reported but agents in Melbourne were able to send supplies from Ballaraat♣ to meet the walkers and no deaths were reported.[93] Although Ho A Low (aka Howloa) who acted as interpreter in the Ayun vs Sage court case did refer to those 'found dead on the way of hunger & thirst'.[94]

That even with an unplanned embarkation at Guichen Bay provisions and support were forthcoming that allowed for a successful ending of the journey demonstrates the high or at least 'business-like' level of organisation involved. As does the successful prosecution of the case that awarded Ayun £4,500. Though this does not mean that Hong Kong merchants were perfectly informed about the Australian colonies and the reference to a shipment of the wrong kind of tea – pouchong rather than congou♦ – would imply that Ayun was perhaps moving into a fresh field of endeavour for himself when he organised the passage of 260 gold seekers to the 'new goldfields.'[95]

♣ 'Ballaraat' was the spelling of Ballarat at this time.
♦ Pouchong is a kind of oolong tea whereas congou is a black tea that was popular in 19th century Australia.

From this court proceeding we learn that Hong Kong based merchants were financing gold seekers as well as exporting goods to the Australian colonies. They did this via contracts with the Europeans owners of ships that involved advances, trade goods and securities of a complex nature. These were contracts they were willing and able to see enforced by the British legal system with which they were familiar in Hong Kong. Despite this familiarity, knowledge of what was happening in colonies such as that of Victoria, at a distance of six months or more turn around in communications, could be patchy.

Thus, it would appear from this case that the Hong Kong merchant Ayun had agreed for Captain Gill to take 260 Chinese passengers to Port Philip even though the captain would be liable to pay £20 per passenger in excess of the *Emma's* tonnage limit (260 tons equals only 26 Chinese passengers tax free). This would have cost more than the $13,500 (around £4,000) advance Gill had received. The calculation is that at least 234 of the passengers on the *Emma* would have been over its 26-passenger limit. This would have meant some £4680 in tax was payable, and each passenger would still have been liable for their individual £10 poll tax. The explanation could be that despite awareness of the new Victorian legislation and taxes in Hong Kong, some confusion still existed that went beyond what was the best tea to export for the Australian market. Sufficient confusion that either Ayun believed Captain Gill's assurances he would or could deliver all the passengers to Port Philip, or that Captain Gill was not aware of his full labilities until he arrived at Adelaide when he made other arrangements. Arrangements which did not however relieve him of his labilities under the charterparty which Ayun was still able to enforce. Assuming it was agents of Ayun who arranged for supplies to be sent from Ballarat to those who found themselves unexpectedly walking with insufficient supplies, then Ayun can be seen as honest but mislead.

This explanation would seem plausible when an account of a controversy over the Victorian tax that took place in Hong Kong in March 1856 is considered. This controversy would have taken place around the time the *Emma*, her owner and her captain were negotiating the charterparty with Ayun. According to this account of the debate:

IMMIGRATION OF CHINESE TO AUSTRALIA. —
For the purpose of helping to remove certain misapprehensions prevalent on this subject in

Hongkong, the *China Mail* of the 13th March; publishes the following: —Three weeks ago attention was drawn in our columns to the vessels on the berth which had been chartered by Chinese for the conveyance of their countrymen to Melbourne, under the impression (or taking the risk) that there no longer existed, any restriction on the trade. Subsequently a representation on the subject was addressed to the Governor by several foreign firms, who pointed out the efficacy of a warning under official sanction; but the Government has not thought fit to adopt even so simple a mode of thwarting a ruinous deception. Some person, however, has endeavoured to remedy this neglect of our rulers by issuing a proclamation, comparatively ineffectual as not bearing the stamp of authority, which has been posted up rather sparingly, and speedily torn down, again, most probably by persons interested in continuing the deception. The subjoined translation is made by a Chinese, and may therefore be considered as conveying the meaning the Chinese attached to the original. Mr. Ya-le, mentioned at the close, may be intended for the Chief Magistrate; but if so, the reference does not supply the authority necessary to give effect to the warning. We may observe, too, that the proclamation is itself calculated to deceive, in telling the Chinese, whose sole intention is to betake themselves to the Victoria gold-diggings, that they may proceed to Sydney or Adelaide, without further informing them of the difficulties they would encounter in proceeding from either of those places to their destination. We regard the landing of Chinese destined for Port Phillip at either of these ports as a subterfuge. "Doctor's money" seems a curious term to use for the sum to be paid for Chinese landed at Melbourne according to law. But it seems it is generally understood to mean head-money (literally body-money, price of the body), and originated in the tax first levied on Chinese in California, under pretext of being for the support of an hospital for their use: —"The captains of some foreign vessels in Hongkong have chartered their ships to Chinese to convey Chinese passengers to Melbourne, Port Phillip. The Chinese do not know the regulations of that place, and this will inform them. The new regulations of Melbourne are for the purpose of preventing the Chinese emigrants going there. To every 10 tons of burden vessels are allowed to carry one passenger, including the captain and the crew, and every passenger must pay £10 doctor's money (head-money). If the captain should land his passengers before he pays the £10 head-money, he will be fined £20. These regulations have been in force since the 11th month of the last English year. Such being the case, what will those captains do with their overloaded passengers? They must pay £20 fine for every surplus passenger besides £10 doctor's money. Are those captains willing to pay that sum? —if not, then each passenger must pay his passage-money and £20 fine, or the captains must sail the ships to some other port and not to Melbourne. You passengers ought to examine these particulars before you pay the bargain-money to the charterers, and save yourselves from being deceived by them. These regulations are established only for the province of Victoria, in Australia, and the port of Melbourne is in that province. Mr. Ya-le says that under these regulations those ships can never get to Port Phillip, but they may proceed to Sydney or Adelaide."—Argus.'[96]

From this account it is clear that various parties in Hong Kong were perfectly aware of the legal situation in Victoria but that each had different purposes in interpreting it to those who wished to travel to the goldfields. Broadly speaking these were, those who wished to encourage (and profit from) such travel, and those who wished to minimise or at least ensure no one suffered unduly from the travel circumstances imposed by the new taxes. Profit versus moral considerations with a hapless government standing somewhere in-between would appear a familiar situation then and now.

Gold seekers perspective

These court cases and debates give us a glimpse into the organisation from the Chinese side, particularly of the merchants for whom the whole enterprise was a form of investment. Even rarer is the view of the ordinary gold seeker loaded onto the ships and embarked at ports with perhaps little idea what was before them. A petition presented in October 1857 to the Victorian legislature arguing against a proposed resident's tax on Chinese goldminers gives us an indication of what their perspective might have been about the walk they had been constrained to undertake:

> It is not the Chinaman's fault but the merchants and captains at Hong Kong who bargain to pay the tax and land us at Port Phillip, but, instead, land us at Guichen Bay, and it is a great hardship to pass overland.' 'We feel it hard, when we have paid the captain, to have to come overland, and many in hunger, others sick, and some die.[97]

Put in even stronger terms is a report from the earlier meeting that produced this petition.

> Then about Chinamen coming from Adelaide and Guichen Bay, and running away from the Government tax. Chinamen do that sometimes, but it is not their fault. They paid £10 tax at Hong Kong to be taken to Australia, and then captain and owner cheat them, and land them at Adelaide. The walk overland is very bad, and causes much suffering. Chinamen would not do it, except Captains cheat them.'[98]

Pon-Sa gave a similar impression of suffering and misinformation when he said: 'Many of their people landed at Guichen Bay. On their road here many of them died of hunger and thirst, and disease, and some hanged themselves. They thought the English would kill them, or take all their money in fines.'[99] Even more directly Chu a Luk wrote that: 'Fully twenty boat-loads of Chinese set sail from Hong Kong with the expectation of landing in Melbourne only to be violently turned on the shore of Guichen Bay to the great detriment of their property and their own personal risk and inconvenience.'[100]

These are rare instances of a Chinese gold seeker expressing a view on their Guichen Bay walk, though Chu a Luk was a missionary speaking in their behalf, and all are speaking in the context of arguing in opposition to a proposed Chinese resident's tax. This tax was partly designed to replace the too easily evaded poll tax and the argument was that any evasions were not necessarily the responsibility of the gold seekers themselves. Thus, the argument from ignorance may be an exaggeration, an exaggeration made more probable given the level of preparedness of many arrivals and the fact that many villages would have contained returned gold seekers able to inform those thinking of going.

Exaggeration or not many of the passengers on these ships were likely to have been misinformed or at least not informed in detail of the prospects in front of them on leaving their families and villages. However, was it the case that arriving unexpectedly at Guichen Bay rather than Port Philip was true for the majority of the many hundreds of ships and many thousands of gold seekers? Certainly, these comments and petitions strongly imply that some at least of the walkers did not have a clear idea beforehand of what their journey entailed and/or that they did not feel in complete control. Thus, while merchants like Ayun based in Hong

Kong were planning as much as they could, it was those actually travelling to the Australian colonies who had to adapt to the circumstances they found on arrival.

(4) A more than usual degree of activity – arrival and departure

The standard image of how the gold seekers from China adapted to Australia is pictured in terms of large groups carrying their supplies on bamboo poles as they walk in lines strung out across the landscape.* This has in fact become the stereotyped image but in at least one instance we have a smaller party organising itself very differently. In this case a 'party of 19 Chinamen have agreed to accompany one another over land from Adelaide, in preference to the Murray and Guichen Bay routes.' And 'for £42' they purchase a 'horse and cart' 'for the conveyance of their luggage'. We know this because two of the party purposely went to the office of the *South Australian Register* to inform them 'that himself and friends should be duly chronicled amongst the "departures"'.♣[101]

---

* See Image 6, p.27.
♣ It is interesting to note that Eric Rolls, *Sojourners*, p.135, mentions this purchase as an example of Chinese being overcharged – converting the £42 into $17,500. Yet there is no hint of the cost being excessive in the report and in fact the comment is made of one informant that 'he spoke English tolerably well, and was evidently one of those whom it would not be easy to deceive in any language.'

The image of the small party with horse and cart would appear exceptional. For the most part we must rely on numerous if tantalisingly vague descriptions of groups of Chinese gold seekers as they passed through various townships. These sightings at Mount Gambier in May and again in July 1856 are typical: 'about 40 Celestials with their tents &c., who' ... 'arrived here and departed on foot, carrying their baggage, which was calculated to weigh about a ton in the aggregate, on their backs.'[102] 'Many of these poor pedestrians seemed quite footsore and exhausted on their arrival here. They carry all their effects with them, slung on the extremities of a bamboo cane in true Chinese fashion.' For the writer their 'uniform good behaviour whilst in encampment' was only marred by their 'national vice, however, of gambling.'[103]

Evolving Routes

The capacity to adapt of the gold seekers can be further seen in the evolution of the routes taken to the goldfields. Having embarked at Adelaide, a number of ways of getting to the Victorian diggings were possible and there appear to have been the two prime routes by mid-1856. The first and most direct route used by those first arriving in 1856 was to take the so-called Tolmer Gold Escort Route or 'Murray route' which ran north of the Grampians into the goldfield districts. This was first pioneered in 1852 and was an improvement on previous routes to help ensure that some of the gold being dug out of Victoria by South Australians would find its way back to South Australia.[104] At almost the same time a government survey team was mapping out the best overland route, including sinking appropriately distanced wells when possible.[105] But alternatives to this route were available and it was reported of the Chinese arrivals that 'the preparations necessary for the entire overland journey on foot are weighed very carefully against the cost of a steam passage to Guichen Bay'.[106] The route, after taking 'steamer or coasting vessel' down to Robe town on Guichen Bay, entailed a shorter walk to the south of the Grampians.[107]

An alternative route involved sticking to the coast via Lake Albert and along the Coorong as far as Salt Creek and Tilley's Flat before turning inland to Naracoorte (Mosquito Plains) and heading towards Mount Arapiles and then onto the goldfields.[108] A variation on this was to cross the Murray River at Wellington and then continue inland, crossing the SA/Victoria border further north but still passing Mount Arapiles before reaching the goldfields.[109] It is difficult to say what proportion of the some 5,000 who disembarked at

Adelaide in 1856 took which route but the bulk seem to have opted for steamers to Robe and then commenced walking the thereby shorten route. There are numerous instances throughout 1856 of steamers 'clearing out coastwise' before arriving with groups of 'Chinese on their way to the diggins in Victoria'.[110]

This route so proving itself that in 1857 most of the gold seekers arrived directly at Robe from Hong Kong, though some also continued to arrive at Adelaide and tranship to Robe.

Once at Guichen Bay there were also numerous routes that could be taken, some based on the season and the weather. Thus - 'All these men arrived in this colony by one or two roads, either by way of Penola and Casterton, or by Mosquito Plains [Naracoorte] and Apsley'.[111] The walkers separating even more once well within Victoria: 'During the last few days 260 Chinamen were travelling towards the gold-fields, by the Horsham and Lexton road, 160 by the Upper Glenelg, a similar number by Casterton and Mount Sturgeon, and nearly 300 were crossing the plains between Streatham and Ballaarat, besides several smaller parties.'[112] By mid-1857: 'A correspondent, writing from Streatham (Fiery Creek), states that since last New Year's Day, 10,000 Chinamen have passed through that township enroute to the various diggings, besides those who come from Guichen Bay by other roads.'[113] A few years later there was a report of '500 of the Chinese landed at Guichen Bay' spreading 'themselves along different roads to the various diggings'.[114] On occasions, perhaps due to flooding, an even more southerly route via Mount Gambier and Portland was also undertaken. This last was a route recommended for the overland telegraph in 1856.[115]

The route from Robe inland is a fairly level one, only very gradually rising and with most tracks winding to follow rivers and creeks. School inspector James Bonwick who was also a keen geologist and who travelled all over western Victoria in the same year as the bulk of the Chinese gold seekers described it: 'The land of the West generally has been raised gradually; though the height of the Wannon district is considerable, the fall is gradual down to the sea coast.'[116] While Tolmer found the 'regular beaten overland road ... is rather circuitous, as it follows the windings of the river'.[117] Father Julian Woods often travelled around this open country using only a compass as 'you could always take the bush without any fear of being stopped by fences.'[118] The main impediment was water or rather too much of it, with the flat country under water in what is today a landscape criss-crossed with drainage ditches. The year the walkers from China began to use the road out of Robe in great numbers it had not improved despite local agitation: 'Great inconvenience is being felt by the settlers on account of the state of the roads leading into the interior. The Reedy Creek is still without a causeway, although a numerously signed petition was presented six months ago upon the subject.'[119]

Image 8: Compass of Father Woods, Mary MacKillop Penola Centre.

71

The landscape

In addition to the roads, the towns the walkers passed in this period would have been little more than a handful of buildings, many new built. Horsham in 1852 for example is described as 'a police station, a store, a blacksmith, and one or two wooden houses' and 'Glenarchy' [sic] as 'about the same size'.[120] While at Penola by 1856 there was a 'new Police Station, Court-House, and Pound recently erected'.[121] And the following year school inspector Bonwick stated that 'Casterton contains nearly a score of dwellings, including two stores, and Chaffey's Hotel; in the latter building the Court House is held.'[122] While nearby Coleraine 'consisted of twenty-five houses' at which a 'new stone schoolroom with suitable master's dwelling is just erected.'[123] When the inspector rode to Dunkeld which 'contained six houses, besides a couple of hotels' in June of 1857 he also found that a 'substantial and commodious National School has been erected' that same year, 'with abundant means for the accommodation of Boarders. Should such appear. Nearly £800 were expended on the building'.[124]

The general landscape would also have been very different in ways hard to imagine nowadays, though this report from just after the walkers passed gives some idea of just how much:

> ... such weather as we have had lately, has been so unfavourable to the growth of native grasses, English grass, wherever it has been sown, has prospered with even more than usual luxuriance. If this is the case, it should certainly add to the extensive sowing of artificial grasses on all good land. By this means, by clearing off fallen timber, and by sub-dividing land into moderate sized paddocks there is no doubt but that the grazing capabilities of the Western District may be increased to an extent at present hardly thought of, ---*Hamilton Spectator*.[125]

The weather was also a major factor in the routes chosen for walking. A winter report of 1856 stated: 'The overland route, though of course very boggy in winter, is by many considered preferable to the Guichen Bay route, which has suffered still more from the effect of the late heavy rains.'[126] Even as far along the route as Dunkeld, some two thirds of the way to the goldfields, it was reported that: 'In summer the mails were brought by means of a spring-cart, but in winter a pack horse had to be used.'[127] Poor weather was certainly the cause of encountering 'some difficulty in prosecuting their journey' for at least one group who made the attempt via Guichen Bay in mid-1856: 'One party, after travelling 16 miles, or as far as the Biscuit Flats, found that they could not without the assistance of animal power proceed further, as the late heavy rains had lodged in this place over an extent of about 12 miles, and to a depth of two or three feet.'[128]

The Murray

Another route taken at first was via the Murray river and it was reported that while many 'have gone overland', 'many have chosen to avail themselves of the Murray packets'.♦[129] Thus, in June 1856 we are told that: 'Arrangements have been made to convey the greater portion of the Chinese passengers per *Jamestown* by the steamer *Leichhardt*, by the Goolwa route and up the Murray, as far as Maiden's Punt, which is only 50 miles from the nearest goldfields.'[130] A route moreover apparently 'well traversed by coaches and other conveyances'.[131] The *Leichhardt* charged 'at the rate of £3 per head' and passengers (or the Chinese ones at least), 'had to provide for themselves, with the exception of wood and water, for which there was a special

---

♦ Navigation on the River Murray having only been established in 1853.

contract made.'[132] Apparently 'a liberal allowance of wood and water' was 'stipulated' as 'necessaries they had most felt the want of during their passage from Hong Kong'. When the time came the ships officers it was reported, 'pointed to the water in the river and the gum-trees on its banks', with the Chinese passengers needing to be convinced that 'the river was fresh water, and the trees were available for fuel.'[133]

Despite its apparent advantages this river route was not one the majority ended up taking and it is not clear why this was the case; perhaps high cost, pressure from the Victorian government, the small numbers the river ferries could take, or unreliability due to being navigable at that time 'only six months' of the year.[134]

> Up to the end of the season of 1856 great difficulties and expense attended the conveyance of goods between Adelaide and the river, as owing to the supposed impracticability of navigating the sea-mouth all articles had to be carried in coasting vessels between Port Adelaide and the inconvenient and dangerous roadstead of Port Elliot ; the communication between which place and the vessels trading on the river was managed by means of

a tramway seven miles in length, extending from Port Elliot to the Goolwa.◆[135]

Certainly, one writer believed Victorian government pressure was responsible:

> The influx of Celestials, via the Murray, has been much discouraged by the Victorian Government, and the steamers no longer convey the denizens of the flowery land to the neighbourhood of the gold-fields.[136]

This same writer included the rather farfetched idea that because the Murray River 'had changed its original bed' this meant that 'steamers coming up the river have to pass through a portion of Victoria' thus giving the Victorians grounds for 'the interference of the authorities'.[137]

New South Wales and Tasmania♣

Another route mentioned was via New South Wales: 'The tax of £10 per head upon each Chinaman, to be paid by the captain of the ship before the celestial emigrants are allowed to land in Victoria, is operating favourably for New South

---

◆ This was a horse drawn tram.
♣ Called Van Diemen's Land officially until the beginning of 1856.

Wales. Two shiploads have, within the last fortnight, come on to Sydney, and many of them have, we understand, joined their companions on the auriferous fields.'[138] If embarking at Sydney this was a long walk to the Victorian goldfields and it seems that some whose 'original intention was to proceed to Port Phillip overland, in order to avoid the capitation tax imposed in the sister colony' instead choose 'to try the gold-fields of the Western Districts.'[139]

Despite the growth of the NSW goldfields some preferred to brave 'the hardships and fatigues of an overland journey' to head for the Victorian just the same.[140] In August 1856 a group of 300 who had 'arrived from Hong Kong per Alfred' embarked at Sydney and chartered the 'screw-steamer *Wonga Wonga*' to take them to Guichen Bay, 'leaving Sydney on Saturday, the 19th inst., at 6 p.m.' and landing 'on Wednesday, the 23rd'.[141] And in early 1857 another group did a similar transhipping, though this time from Launceston in Tasmanian to Guichen Bay.[142] Some were still doing this a couple of years later, crossing the Murray River despite the efforts of the Chinese Protector to collect what by then was only a £1 residents tax.[143]

A Tasmanian route was by no means a regular one and in fact seems another instance of less than forthright dealing by ships captains and owners. The passengers on the *Louisiana* left Hong Kong believing they were headed to either Port Philip or if not, the cost of their onward leg would be covered. On being told to leave the ship in Tasmania at the end of 1856 the local magistrates were appealed to and extended court proceedings seem to have begun. In court Captain Gardner was able to prove that only 14 of his passenger's contracts (within the tonnage limit) specified 'Port Philip' while the others merely said 'Australia' as their destination. As Tasmania was considered within the definition of 'Australia' the case was dismissed. The misled passengers, which included at least one with a 'blue calico umbrella' and another who 'carried a fan' and a 'self-satisfied air and carefully arranged dress' that led him to being described as a 'dandy', eventually arranged to have their heavier luggage sent to the goldfields via Melbourne while they took the steamers *Tamar* and *Vixen* to Guichen Bay.♦[144]

♦ This case was impacted by the tonnage restrictions, a similar case, also involving Tasmania as equating 'Australia', had occurred before such restrictions in 1854.

Direct to Guichen Bay

The bypassing of Port Phillip via Tasmania resulted in 50 Chinese gold seekers in 'the schooner Vixen' arriving in early 1857 at Robe on the same day as a 'new method of shipping Chinese emigrants for Port Robe, instead of for Port Adelaide' began.[145] This was heralded by the arrival of the 'ship *Land o' Cakes*, 560 tons from Hongkong' 'landing 350 Chinese, and taking 36 more on with her to Melbourne.'✦[146] The significance of the *Land o'Cakes* was that it had sailed direct from Hong Kong to Guichen Bay.✚[147] Subsequent arrivals of these larger ocean-going ships throughout 1857 would greatly increase the numbers passing through the small port of Robe. In fact, the Victorian Parliament was told it resulted in numbers 'nearly double' to 11,403 by mid-1857 or perhaps 14,675 for the whole of 1857.[148]

✦ Actually, it was less than 300 Chinese passengers.
✚ By contrast the first ship direct from London to Robe did not arrive until the end of 1857.

Image 9: Guichen Bay, author photo, 2022.

It was this ramping up of numbers at Robe in 1857 that is the prime focus of most accounts of the Chinese walkers, despite the many hundreds that had also arrived the previous year. Interestingly an eyewitness report describes the arrival of the *Land o'Cakes* and a number of other ships with Chinese passengers as generating only a 'more than usual degree of activity' and even so couples this with 'the greatly-increased traffic in wool' as the cause.[149] One consequence of these Hong Kong ships sailing directly to Robe is that the Adelaide papers had to obtain their international news via this small town: 'We have Hongkong journals to the 24th January, brought to Guichen Bay by the Challenge, and obligingly forwarded to us from thence by Mr. Melville.'♥[150]

Nonetheless, the increase in numbers was great and in March 1857 for example the arrival around the same time of: 'Three vessels, the Investigator, Oracle, and W Miles' brought 'about 1,500 emigrants from China' into Guichen Bay.[151] Even more dramatically – 'From a return laid before the Legislative Assembly of South Australia, it appears that between the 17th January and the 1st May, 22 ships have landed 10,157 Chinese passengers at Guichen Bay.'[152] Even stretched over months this is a large number, while in May 1857 it was reported that Robe 'had 3,000 Chinese encamped round the town' after 'four more ships' arrived.[153] Presumably not counting the coastal screw steamers, 42 'vessels' were reported to have entered Robe in 1857, at least 31 of these carrying Chinese gold seekers.[154]

Reaction

While the large numbers landing must have put great pressure on scarce resources at the small port, Robe seems to have dealt with it more calmly than subsequent accounts

---

♥ Mr. Melville was the customs official at Robe.

of 'invasion' would allow. The Governor of South Australia appears to have summed up the situation best:

> The great numbers in which they landed at Robe Town–as many as 924 arriving in one ship–induced me to station a small military detachment there; but I am bound to say in behalf of this singular race that, considering the circumstances of their arrival and the extortion and provocation to which they were occasionally subjected, they have hitherto manifested in their conduct considerable forbearance and respect for the law, conducting themselves generally with decorum and propriety.[155]

This small military force of 25 was delayed in its leaving for Guichen Bay as the steamer *Burra Burra* they first attempted to take was full – with Chinese passengers.[156] This casual attitude to the movement of soldiers and the Governor's feeling that no problem was forthcoming from the Chinese arrivals seems to have been the consensus opinion in South Australia at the time. Not that more hysterical (bordering on modern 'fake news') perspectives were totally absent, with one writer to the *Adelaide Observer* – who signed himself "Anglo-Australian" – even insisting that many of the 'arrivals in the past two years have not been inhabitants of

China Proper, but natives of Manchouria, a district in which Russian influence is considerable'. As such they could be 'tampered with by the emissaries of the Colossus' which was of course preparing to 'make a descent, upon his Australian quarry'.[157]

The switch to chartering ships directly to Guichen Bay was certainly dramatic but in general did not inspire fears of Russian invasion. From another legal dispute we learn that the option of either Adelaide or direct to Guichen Bay was at least sometimes left open. This was another case of a ship's captain (this time of the *Estrella do Norte*) apparently not fulfilling the 'charter-party', this one signed with a Hong Kong merchant named 'Lum Sing'.[158] Under its terms if embarkation took place at Adelaide, then either the captain would organise a coastal steamer to Guichen Bay or repay the equivalent fare. It was the repayment of this fare that had been estimated at £3 per person that was in dispute.[159]

> The terms of the charter party were that the passengers should be taken to Adelaide, and thence by steam to Guichen Bay; or, if this were impracticable, the amount of their passage money, which had been estimated at £3 a head, should be paid to them. With this understanding separate contracts had been made at Hongkong between

Lum Sing and 242 Chinese, to provide them with passages for 80 dollars each.[160]

(5) Because there was no penal clause – the official response

We have seen the response and adaptability of the Hong Kong merchants and the Chinese gold seekers as they re-drafted charterparties and organised supplies for the longer routes to the Victorian goldfields. But what was the response of the Victorians who had created this situation when it was recognised that due to its narrow framing 'the law could not be applied to arrivals overland from Adelaide or Sydney.'[161] The question: Are we 'in danger of being overrun from Adelaide and Sydney?' had been raised during the Victorian assembly debates on the legislation but had generally been dismissed as inconceivable, or as easily dealt with should it happen.[162]

Surprise

When large numbers of Chinese gold seekers did begin to arrive via Adelaide and Sydney surprisingly the Victorian administration was caught by surprise. So much so that it was not apparently until June of 1856, many months after numerous walkers had entered the Victorian goldfields from South Australia, that the Victorian police attempted to do anything:

Another party, who had got to the confines of the Victorian territory, were, we are informed, arrested by the police of Victoria, and the men driving their drays were arrested and confined under a charge of having violated the Customs laws of that colony. However, the vigilant officers by whom the drivers were arrested almost immediately afterwards discovered that they could not on any pretence whatever detain their prisoners, and they were consequently discharged, but not before the unfortunate Chinese, whose luggage they were conveying, were placed in a situation of many discomforts.[163]

Thus, the Victorian police rather belatedly discovered they had no power in the matter. Instead, one of the first reactions, by some at least, was a realisation of 'the injudicious nature of the heavy poll-tax imposed' and the Victorian Chamber of Commerce even passed a 'resolution condemnatory of the law'. Some of this concern was practical: 'Our revenue has therefore been mulcted of upwards of a hundred thousand pounds for passengers' fees,'[164] A South Australian newspaper was more condemnatory, under the title 'Barbarian Legislation':

> The attempt of the legislators of Victoria to stop the progress of civilization with a poll-tax—to levy a duty upon flesh and blood, as though they were marketable commodities—has turned out as complete a failure as it deserved to be.[165]

As well as the problem of arrival by means other than a Victorian port, the enforcement of the tonnage restriction also proved difficult due to ambiguity as to how it should be calculated. In a number of cases ship captains seem to have been able to have attempts to fine them for carrying too many Chinese passengers dismissed.[166] In fact, while not always successful, a number of captains continued to try and carry more than this limit arguing ignorance in some cases and even that they 'did not care for any colonial act which had been or could be, passed' but preferred 'imperial' laws.[167]

New Taxes

The debate dragged and it became obvious that: 'These Acts were, however, very defective, simply because there was no penal clause to enforce their operation. They were also defective inasmuch as they did not provide for those Chinese who came overland to the colony.'[168] An interesting aspect of the debate on legislation originally designed to reduce the numbers of Chinese people entering the colony was that it often centred on the supposed loss of revenue this evasion entailed. This switch in focus eventually lead not to a tightening of enforcement but the introduction by the end of 1857 of a new tax. This was not an entry tax but a resident's tax which could be levied on any Chinese person regardless of the route taken to enter the colony. Further, this new tax was to be enforced by an official designated the 'Chinese Protector' whose funding was to be provided by this tax.

By August 1858, after colonies had introduced its own poll tax, the residents tax enforcement was also considered 'most unsatisfactory'.[169] The introduction of this new tax had been strongly opposed by the Chinese miners living and working in Victoria. Collection depended apparently on the willingness of people to pay it and 'should John obstinately refuse to be thus frightened out of his money, he is allowed to go at liberty'.[170] While no doubt speculation, one observer reported:

> A barked tree, marked in Chinese characters, may now be seen on the road to Wodonga, and we believe the purport of the inscription is to caution all future mobs of Chinamen to persist in telling the English devils that they have no money.[171]

This situation continued and the various discriminatory taxes continued to be avoided or resisted whenever possible. In 1862, after the South Australian repeal of its poll tax led to a small recurrence of the Guichen Bay walk; perhaps disappointingly small for the SA Chamber of Commerce which had supported the repeal.[172] One group ended up having a 'spell' in Ararat gaol.[173] A few months later, out of a group of 500 only 88 were taken up by the Victorian police to be 'fined each of them $L1$, or a month's imprisonment also in Ararat jail'.♦ Opting for imprisonment they all seemed 'happy enough' after 'rest and food' in the tents provided.[174] Though a little after this it was reported that '53 of them have been released by their brother celestials £5 each having been paid'.[175]

In 1863, a group off the *Independence* reported that 'the captain of the vessel led them to understand that, 'if land in Melbourne or Sydney, Chinaman would have to pay £10 each, but if land at Guichen Bay pay nothing.'[176] Though what benefit the captain derived from misleading them at this stage is unclear. On being enlightened regarding residing in Victoria, which would require them to pay £4 each regardless of how they entered the colony, 'they

---

♦ $L1$ – one guinea or £1 10 schillings.

collected £40 and sent ten of their number off to Ballaarat.[177] The remaining 'forty-Chinamen' were 'committed to the Portland Jail for non-payment of the capitation tax. The men are now employed daily from 8 a.m. to 5 p.m., in the Botanical Gardens'.[178]

Round Two

The walkers of 1862 and 1863 were seemingly subject to a game of chance, such as these: 'An importation of "Celestials" arrived here on Good Friday from Guichen Bay on their way to Ballarat. They numbered between 60 and 70, and after staying a few hours for the purpose of visiting the butcher and Boniface; again, started on their road towards Casterton.'[179] Soon after:

> The unjustly severe and partial manner in which the Chinese are at present affected by Victorian law was forcibly brought under the notice of the Wickliffe inhabitants on Saturday last. While looking on one of those ant-like spectacles, a moving mob of Chinese Immigrants, attractive from variety of garb, and the toiling so happily under unconscionable burdens. A new interest was suddenly lent to the scene by two mounted constables galloping into the town and after a brief consultation with our local force, by a quick and hostile movement being

made to the front of John's Line, which was gradually shut up into a solid mass. The Chinese, apparently neither surprised nor disconcerted, were then informed they were prisoners of the Crown for evading payment of the entrances rate. After this "rounding up" (for the meek compliance of the Chinese gave sheep-like aspect to the transaction). The flock was passed out in single file for counting, and then quietly "folded" for the night. These sixty-eight men of China being kept safely, were taken next morning to Ararat by four constables. Englishmen, who looked on and remembered that what was criminal in these Chinamen would be innocent in Spaniards and men of Morocco must have felt somewhat ashamed, and that such a law was discordant with the British boast of impartial fair play. No censure was intended upon the constables who had this unpleasant duty to discharge. They executed their task as mildly and considerately as men could do.[180]

Worse than a spell in gaol was arriving too late in the season, the *Maria Bradford* arrived at Guichen Bay on August 1 1863:

CHINAMEN AT THE AVENUE [a pastoral run near Penola]. -A correspondent- writing to a gentleman in this place says:-There are three hundred and fifty Chinamen here, and they propose going overland to Ballarat. I am doing all I can to get the police to interfere, because I am sure that half that number would never reach Penola alive. The strongest men would never wade ten miles through boggy country up to the arm-pits in water. That these Chinamen should have been put upon the Penola track at this season of the year, reflects but little credit upon the guides. It is a generally known fact that every year about this time a great many miles of the Penola and Mosquito Plains roads are under water, and often travelled by horsemen with great difficulty. To put these Chinamen on either of these tracks shows a great want of judgment. More especially as they could travel along the Mount Gambier Road, past Warkyine; Mr G. Glen's and Narrowneck almost dry shod, and reach their destination without making any great detour in so doing. We trust "John" may be delivered from his troubles and put upon the best road at last.[181]

Evidently some on the *Mary Bradford* knew the walk would be too difficult at this time and chose to take the steamer *Havilah* to Sydney instead as she carried 'a number of Chinese as passengers' who arrived on the 'Mary Bradford, from Hong Kong' who were 'bound for Sydney'.[182] But not the majority:

Between three and four hundred Chinese passed through Hamilton yesterday on their way from Guichen Bay to Ballarat. They were recent arrivals from China, but some among them had been in the colony before, and had returned to China. These men, of course, were "doing" the overland journey to save the capitation tax. They were unmolested by the police of Hamilton, but it is not unlikely that they will be bailed up at Wickliffe, where it will be remembered some months ago a number of their compatriots were arrested and sent to Ararat gaol.[183]

This is apparently what did happen, but only to some from the same ship:

The Ararat Advertiser of Friday last says :— 'We received an addition to our population on Wednesday, in the shape of seventy Chinamen, who travelled overland to this place from Guichen Bay; they are part of a mob of between 300 and 400 that landed at the latter place, the remainder have gone on to the Ovens and to some of the other gold-fields.'[184]

The arrivals after South Australia repealed its own poll tax were subject to the new resident's tax, intermittent police enforcement and it seems poorer weather. As well, contrary to the well organised groups of 1856 and 1857 those of 1862

93

and 1863 who also arrived in Robe seem much less well equipped. Most at least arrived in the drier and cooler autumn, but those who arrived off the *Mary Bradford* in a gale faced much colder and wetter conditions:

> The Chinamen were all safely landed by Messrs. Ormerod's boats at a reasonable rate, the vessel took its departure the following day for Sydney. The Chinamen started on Thursday last for Ballarat. They purpose going by way of Penola. How they will get across the flats at this period of the year and in their present condition, is a source of anxiety to those who can feel even for a Chinaman. Travelling on horseback is attended, with no little danger and difficulty. We can only hope no accidents will happen to them.[185]

A month later their arrival was reported:

> The march is a long one, and the inclemency of the season seems to have told severely upon the poor strangers. One of them died at Ballarat a few hours after his arrival, and another-it is reported-has since died at the Chinese camp on Ballarat.[186]

(6) Boats at a reasonable rate – what it all cost

The reference above of a "sympathetic' observer" – one who could 'feel even for a Chinaman' – to 'boats at a reasonable rate' raises the broader question of costs. The cost of this mass movement from the villages of the Pearl River Delta to the gold fields of Victoria and the associated question of fair costs and overcharging, not to mention failure to provide what was paid for is one that arises again and again in this history. The fare from Hong Kong, the taxes to be paid, the cost of provisions, guides, coastal steamers, and even the price of being transferred to the shore at Robe were all naturally of significance to those who paid, or who eventually needed to repay, this money.

For Pearl River Delta villagers hoping to make their and their families fortunes on the gold fields, the various costs incurred on the way were significant. In the context of the Guichen Bay walk, costs included many extras that those who arrived at Port Philip and made their shorter way to the goldfields did not incur. These outlays included fares for the steamers they transhipped to get to Guichen Bay or fees to get from the Hong Kong ships that went direct to Guichen

95

Bay to get to the jetty at Robe, the supplies required to walk the longer distances, and the guides and/or drivers required for those unfamiliar with the terrain or to carry the heavier gear and provisions. These costs were presumably calculated by the sponsors and provided to the organised groups but of course any plan can go astray and unexpected costs or exorbitant charges might be met only with difficulty.

Earlier it was seen that $80Mex or perhaps £20 was the cost per passenger of a chartered vessel from Hong Kong to Adelaide or Melbourne. This fee did not include provisions and water which were provided by the passengers or their backers. Once at Adelaide a range of other costs had to be negotiated including supplies, drays, and guides/drivers. If going to Robe the cost of the coastal steamer or, if the ship arrived directly, the cost of boats to land passengers at a bay with insufficient depth for the larger ships had also to be found.

For those who arrived in Adelaide in 1856 it was noted that: 'Frequent discussions and calculations are engaged in with uncommon earnestness, and the preparations necessary for the entire overland journey on foot are weighed very carefully against the cost of a steam passage to Guichen Bay, by which a pedestrian trip to the gold-diggings of Victoria may be shortened so considerably.'[187] The newly commissioned steamers *Burra Burra* and *White Swan*, equipped with the latest screw technology, were available and provided passage to Guichen Bay at around £4 per person in 'steerage'.[188] It was this amount that needed to be weighed against the extra time and provisions needed for the longer walk. There does not seem to have been any hint of overcharging when it came to these coastal steamers and the costs seem to have been widely known and advertised.[189] Even when a group of 300 Chinese gold seekers arrived in Sydney and chartered the *Wonga Wonga* for £1200 'to convey them from Sydney to Guichen Bay' this worked out at the similar rate of £4 each' for the four day journey.[190] Though prices were rising and in that same month it was announced that the 'three regular trading steamers between Adelaide and Melbourne have united in raising their fares' and consequently the 'first-class passage-money is raised from £8 5s. to £9 9s. and the steerage from £4 to £5.'[191]

Wages & Prices

It the always difficult to appreciate what costs and prices in the past actually meant. Though it is worth noting that the South Australian Governor, when discussing in 1857 the

Colony of South Australia's own restrictions on Chinese immigration, felt this came at the loss of 'large sums expended by the Chinese here'.[192] The Governor was considering the total spending of thousands. On a more individual level, first class in a steamer was more than a month's wage for a seaman. While the somewhat lesser steerage fee was still a fair proportion of such a worker's wage:

> Seaman's Wages—The wages of seamen at the Port have not differed materially for the past eight months, but at the opening of the Murray it is most likely wages will increase. The Estrella do Norte shipped hands at £6 per month for able seamen, which is the usual rate given for long voyages. The coasting trade only give £5 for able seamen, but there are not very many at present wanting berths.[193]

While seamen's wages included board and lodging, a skilled worker such as a carpenter or cabinetmaker without board or lodging was reported in 1856 to be earning 10 to 12 schillings per day in Adelaide. This would make the steamer cost equivalent to around a week's earnings.[194] Of course such a cost to a Chinese villager was even greater but would have been weighed against his hopes of future income from gold seeking.

```
              LABOUR MARKET.
Per annum, with board and   Engineers, 10/ to 15/
       lodging:              Ironfounders, 17/ to 20/
Domestic servants—           Labourers, 5/ to 7/
  Male, £10 to £50           Masons, 10/ to 11/
  Female, £10 to £20         Millers, 10/ to 12/
Farm servants—               Miners, 5/ to 7/
  Marr. Couples, £40 to £60  Painters, &c., 10/
  Single Men, £35 to £50     Plasterers, 10/ to 12/
Shepherds, £35 to £40        Saddlers, 10/ to 12/
Per week, with board and     Shoemakers, 7/ to 10/
       lodging:              Shoeing Smiths, 10/ to 14/
Butchers, £2 to £2 10s.      Tanners, &c., 8/ to 10/
Bakers, £1 10s. to £2 2s.    Watch and Clock Makers,
Bullockdrivers, 16/ to 20/     10/ to 12/
Confectioners, £2 2s.        Wheelwrights, 10/ to 12/
Per day, without board and       Piece-work:
       lodging:              Brickmakers, 15/ to 20/ ℔
Blacksmiths, 10/ to 12/        1,000
Bricklayers, 10/ to 11/      Sawyers, 13/ ℔ 100 cedar,
Cabinetmakers, 10/ to 12/      9/ ℔ 100 deal
Carpenters, 10/ to 12/       Tailors, /10 ℔ hour
Carriagemakers, 12/          Reaping, 15/ to 20/ ℔ acre,
Coopers, 8/ to 10/             with wine or ale
      RATE OF SEAMEN'S WAGES AT PORT ADELAIDE.
   The rate of wages for foreign ships has had an upward
tendency for the last few weeks, and now stands at £6.
The pay given by extracolonial vessels has not yet been
raised above £5, but £6 is offered for coasting voyages.
   January 31, 1856
```

Image 10: Labour market 1856, *South Australian Register*, 5 February 1856, p.2.

Sail or Steam

Despite this cost, not all seem to have spent as much time considering the options and some arrived at Adelaide already prepared to tranship to a coastal steamer and make their way via Robe. Thus, in May 1856 some 250 people 'transhipped from the *Cornwall*' to the *White Swan* apparently directly without even landing at Port Adelaide.[195] Not all took the modern steamers and various 'schooners' also took people on to Guichen Bay.[196] Sailing vessels would usually be expected to take longer and thus more provisions were needed. An 1856 advertisement for 'steam vessels' and 'sailing vessels' provided the same steerage (£4 5s.) rates from Adelaide to Melbourne, however, under sailing vessels is an additional cut rate of £2 for Chinese passengers if they are 'providing themselves'.[197]

There was greater risk in taking a schooner, as can be seen in the journey of the *Gem* in August 1856. In July that year the steamer *Burra Burra* was reported to have 'accomplished in fifty-one hours,' the Adelaide to Melbourne run, including a Guichen Bay stop to embark her Chinese passengers.[198] A month later there was much concern when the schooner *Gem* failed to arrive at Guichen Bay with its 110 Chinese passengers. The *Gem* 'experienced three weeks of most severe weather' that turned this trip of hours into a three-week ordeal with the schooner 'compelled to run into Portland [in Victoria] for provisions and water'.♦ [199] Even after this the *Gem* failed to make it all the way back to Guichen Bay and finally landed the Chinese gold seekers at Rivoli Bay, not far off but necessarily within the tax free South Australian borders.[200] Private Ewens, a constable based at Robe, also reported 104 'poor wretches' when the schooner *Fame* took three weeks to arrive.[201] Not that taking a steamer avoided all hardships as when the *White Swan* 'sailed for Guichen Bay on Saturday evening with 300 Chinese' arriving 'at Guichen Bay on Sunday; but, as the weather was very rough, did not land her passengers till Monday.'[202]

Getting ashore

By 1857 all these considerations had reached Hong Kong including the realisation that larger vessels could use Guichen Bay and so the majority of ship arrivals that year were chartered directly to Guichen Bay. While this eliminated the cost of the steamer or schooner from Adelaide

---

♦ Apparently, the captain was brought before the police in Portland and threatened with being fined for his excess passengers to which he could only plead 'stress of weather'.

it still left the price of getting from ship to shore at a port without a jetty capable of taking these larger vessels out of Hong Kong. This was a procedure that caused some comment either because of a shortage of small boats to take so many off at a time, rough weather on occasions, impatience of Captains to get their ships away for fear of damage, or a general belief on the part of passengers that their fare should include the cost of being put ashore.*[203] No doubt some or even all factors operated at times.

Within a week in late May 1857 at least five ships arrived at Robe carrying over 2,300 passengers. According to report the Chinese passengers were charged 'from ten to twenty shillings' to disembark despite the fact that 'eleven boats have been licensed during the last month'.[204] This may well have been one source of the 'extortion and provocation' referred to by the Governor.[205] The Sub-Collector at Robe gave a similar account, reporting that:

> ... the boatmen charged the Chinese most exorbitant prices for landing varying from five to ten shillings per head and many made enough money to buy a boat so that

---

* Despite several shipwreck's, many maintained Guichen Bay was 'a place of safe anchorage, and they find the obelisk of great service as a land-mark'.

we had quite a flotilla of fine boats, the exactions of the boatmen often led to disturbances and the Chinese knives were unsheathed but no serious affray took place, …[206]

The police reported 10/- as 'the usual hire' when in August 1857 passengers coming off the 'Sanlsette' (Sansette) refused at first to pay, apparently having been informed by 'the Capt. of the vessel' that they would be landed for 1/-. The magistrate was called but 'the Chinese seeing the boatmen determined paid the hire viz. 10/- & were all landed peacefully by ½ past 9 P.M.'[207]

Certainly, the Government Resident at Port Robe felt these charges were too high and he wrote to the Trinity Board [overseeing maritime safety], 'complaining of the extortion practised by the boatmen upon the Chinese passengers arriving at Guichen Bay, and requesting that the Board would, if they possessed the power, make such regulations as would prevent the same'. While the Board 'were of opinion that it would be desirable to protect the Chinese from imposition' they felt that 'the trade to the port in question would cease' before any new law 'could come into operation'.[208] This was presumably in reference to the likely introduction of South Australia's own poll tax which did indeed halt 'the trade' by the following year.[209]

Certainly, these rates are much higher than those reported for the 1862 and 1863 arrivals, though whether this was due to Trinity Board intervention or not is unclear. Thus, we are told that on 'Monday noon, the ship *Buonavista*, arrived from Hongkong, bringing 350 Chinamen. In the evening part of them were landed, and the remainder next morning by Port Robe boats; they paid 3s. each for being landed.' While a lesser charge, it would seem past experience of the cost of this procedure had led to a written pre-payment scheme under which 'the passengers (Chinese) held agreements entered into by those interested in the vessel, setting forth that they were to be conveyed, catered for, and landed at the Port of Guichen Bay, in consideration of having received 28 dollars from each.' This agreement was in both Chinese and English but did not avail in preventing payment of 'over £50 to be landed, when, by the agreement entered into they should have been landed free'.[210] We don't know what arguments may have taken place in Robe that night but the next year we do have the perhaps penitent observation that the 'Chinamen were all safely landed by Messrs. Ormerod's boats at a reasonable rate'.[211] Whatever rate that might had been.

Supplies and Guides

Getting ashore, whether at Adelaide or Guichen Bay was of course only the first step on the long walk to the goldfields themselves. A walk that required sufficient provisions to last at least three weeks by most accounts, though there is no clear idea of what these provisions might have cost. As usual we are reliant in European observers and the cost that they mostly observed was that charged by the guides or drivers, the distinction is not always clear or perhaps relevant. One observer confidently reported that the 'expense of a Chinaman from Guichen Bay to Ballaarat is about four pounds, and the trip occupies above twenty days.'[212] If this was the cost of a guide/driver of drays only, then the cost of provisions must be added. Another reported that the 'cost of the journey overland from Guichen Bay to Bendigo was somewhat under £5 each.' This was compared to that from Melbourne to Bendigo of 'about £2 per head.'[213]

We have accounts of both provisions and guides/drivers being arranged in Adelaide. But this is less clear in Robe perhaps because most of the provisions for the walk were

105

carried on the ship and by 1857 the route had been taken sufficiently often that non-Chinese guides were no longer needed. Thus, in Adelaide in April 1856 after enquiries had 'elicited various offers from carriers and others', one 'teamster' offered to convey 150 people and 'their provision, tents, and baggage, at £2 per head.'[214] This would have given the teamster £300 for some three weeks work. Only a few months later it was reported that the 'remuneration the guides receive is ten shillings per head'.[215] Certainly a substantial difference. While the drivers involved in the Glen Osmond dispute in June 1856 had been 'engaged at £2 per week and their rations for eight weeks certain'.[216] This is higher but not extravagantly so when compared to the 16 to 20 schilling per week including board and lodging reported for 'Bullock drivers' at Adelaide in 1856.[217]

A group that must have already been on the road for some time before the Glen Osmond dispute, paid their guide £1 per head, which came to £80 total.[218] Once closer to the goldfields it was possible and perhaps more desirable in the hillier terrain to hire carriers and Chandler reports he charged £1 per man to take 'a lot of Chinese who had come overland to evade the poll tax' from Alma to Campbell's Creek, a little more than 50 kilometres.[219] While Edward

Hearne from just across the Victorian border reported: 'He sent his brother and another man with a team of bullocks to convey to Ballarat the goods, of one party of Chinese, who paid him £60 for the service.'[220]

Were these reasonable rates? It is always difficult to gage how expensive a cost such as '£1 per man' was, especially at a time of labour shortage and with the option of gold digging and its chances of higher returns. One report was of 'rather more than £3 per week as the average return to each digger.' 'Wages are what we have stated them to be £1 per day as a rule; the lowest that are paid being £4 a week. No digger will work in Beechworth under £1 per day, and not long at that.'[221] If these accounts are correct then a '£1 per man' cost would be hefty but not exorbitant.

Whatever the fee charged the transport of large groups was not an easy thing as this account demonstrates:

> About six hundred Chinese arrived yesterday overland from Guichen Bay. Five bullock drays were filled with their luggage, and from all appearances they were a decent, healthy-looking lot of fellows. The conductors of the expedition admitted they were peaceable and orderly on the road till they got within about thirty miles of

Ballarat, when they attempted to leave the drays, and took off a large portion of their baggage. After travelling about eight miles, on nearing a police station, they returned it, and pursued their journey in the ordinary way. On making further enquiries, we ascertained that they had been nearly four weeks on the road, although the weather was fine, and the country good; and it was not until tired out with the slow progress made, and the shortness of provisions, that they became impatient, and determined to push on. On long and tedious overland expeditions like the one in question, the drivers are bound to use all diligence with so large a body of men entirely unacquainted with our language, and altogether of different temperaments and dispositions. The most fatal consequences might ensue if they fancied, they were suffering from any cause within the control of the Europeans conducting them.'[222]

Such consequences did occur and sometimes a difference of opinion arose quickly, as in early 1857 when it was reported that the 'last troupe of Chinamen who left for the overland journey had some misunderstanding with the man who had engaged to act as their guide, and, yesterday, returned to Adelaide to settle their differences'.[223] A more fatal consequence of disagreement was related a few years later of a group leaving Guichen Bay when as a result 'one of the drays was upset, causing the death of one of the Chinese, besides severely, if not fatally, injuring two others'. One of the draymen was also injured and was 'in a most precarious state'. Not unreasonably 'the Chinese had assumed a most threatening attitude'.[224] An unusual feature of this report is that the group was reported as heading from Guichen Bay not to the goldfields but to Adelaide.

It is in the nature of things that disputes and fatalities are more likely to be reported and certainly many walks are described without incident such as when they were 'in charge of a pilot well acquainted with the best road.'[225] We must always be cognisant of the fact that reliance is on European observers who generally are not sympathetic to the Chinese gold seekers and nearly always ignorant. Simple misreporting and/or exaggeration was also common as when the Glen Osmond dispute, which was reported in detail in Adelaide as largely due to theft by one of their parties, became a case of threats against the guides for this theft by the time the (garbled) report reached the Victorian goldfields.♦

♦ See pp.51-54 above.

(7) The whole atmosphere was Chinese – humping the swag

Having seen how well planned at least some, if not all, the arriving groups were, including their arriving usually at the right season, we can now look at how the actual walks were conducted. As before we are reliant on European observers who did not hesitate to display their sense of superiority towards anyone perceived as different. Still, a sense of the organisation and equipage can be gathered from what are often eyewitness reports. Thus, we are told of the departure from Adelaide in April 1856 of 'some hundreds of Chinamen proceeding with their luggage enroute overland to the diggings. The drays on which the heavier luggage was conveyed also afforded accommodation to a number ... The main body, however, were on foot...' It was noted that many were in 'the garb of English sailors' or a 'combination of Oriental and colonial habiliments.' Their 'conical basket hats' and the 'poles borne on their shoulders' were also noted. Also noted was that some carried 'umbrellas' that were considered 'articles likely to sell to advantage on the journey'.[226]

A little later, in June 1856 we have another detailed eyewitness account of the completion of the journey:

> On April 8th a party of one hundred and fifty Chinese left Adelaide for Ballaarat. Their escort, under the command of Lionel Edwards, late a carter on the Port-road, consisted of five men, each in charge of a two-horse dray, for the conveyance of their food, cooking utensils, and general baggage. The average rate of traveling was twelve miles per day. They arrived at the Avoca diggings on the evening of May 16. … reached Ballaarat in high spirits, strong and healthy, having gained wonderfully upon the journey in flesh and general condition.[227]

Thus, in this group anyway, there was one cart per 30 men to carry baggage and they moved at a modest pace that took a little over five weeks walking. This group may have been particularly well organised as we are also told the man in charge 'had for several years' not only lived in South Australia but 'had amassed a considerable sum'. And it was he who had 'induced this large party of his fellow-countrymen to migrate with him to the goldfields'. Obviously not all groups could be so fortunate and this same group passed 'the grave of several defunct Celestials, their less fortunate precursors'.[228]

Chandler – who was himself a carrier – reported a much lower ratio of wagons to walkers: 'I met between six and seven hundred coming overland from Adelaide. They had four wagons carrying their sick, lame and provisions.'[229] It is not clear if being accompanied by a dray was standard practice in every case as many descriptions only focus on the walkers: 'Each man carried a load of about forty pounds weight, equally divided, and suspended from the ends of a bamboo a few feet in length, balanced on the shoulder.'[230] Would Robe have been able to supply numerous drays unless special provision was made? It was a centre for wool export at the time so perhaps it could have. Though references to drays and Robe are absent.

Detailed descriptions are rare perhaps because the sheer numbers and exotic appearance of the Chinese walkers was enough to occupy the mind of most observers. As a result, the Chinese gold seekers made quite an impact, especially as they seemed to prefer to walk in single file (perhaps due to their long bamboo shoulder poles) which meant they were strung out along the landscape for many kilometres.

Numbers in the hundreds were not unusual and with the arrival of several ships at the same time at Robe in mid-1857, thousands were often on the road at any one time in such numbers 'that as many as 4,000 have passed by one station near Harrow, within the last month.'[231] Clothes, hats and language all made up more than sufficient to make an impact in addition to sheer numbers as in this account of their passage:

> They were nearly all dressed similarly, having on broad cane hats, yellowish coats, and loose blue pantaloons. Each one had a long bamboo over his shoulder from which depended two well stuffed bags; and as they passed along in Indian file, some ten or fifteen feet apart, the front rank was past the residence of Mr Train before the last of them was past the cottage of Mr Lynch, the distance between the two places being fully a mile and a quarter.[232]

Another eyewitness reports that 'they were cleanly in their persons, and their countenances were intelligent.'[233]

The impact must have been intense and according to Julian Woods in Robe in early 1857:

There were Chinese men, Chinese cloths, Chinese baskets and old thick soled felt shoes of the veritable Chinese pattern, Chinese trays, work bags, chessmen, paper knives etc etc to be seen on every side. The whole atmosphere was Chinese ...[234]

School inspector Bonwick saw similar as he traveled west from Casterton: 'For several miles I rode upon the Chinese track, and discovered several relics of the Tea land.'[235]

Those who had brought things to sell may have done well in Adelaide, but Robe must have been a disappointment. In any event Woods when travelling along the same route from Robe to Penola as the gold seekers reported:

The road to Penola was like Guichen Bay in its Chinese aspect. Both sides of the track were marked by stray articles of clothing or baggage indicating how like a retreating army fatigue had made the Chinese abandon their goods one by one.'[236] Their passing left many objects 'both useful and ornamental but these were too numerous to attract attention and really the population of the district was then so scattered and small that there was no one to collect them. There they lay in the mournful solitude of the heaths and plains and the bark of many a tree was traced all over with Chinese characters containing warnings or advice or information for subsequent parties.[237]

The gold seekers from the villages of the Pearl River Delta came well equipped, as this account of a group arriving at Port Phillip before the poll tax was introduced describes:

> They had a very large number of baskets, with a small proportion of small casks, boxes, cases, and tubs, in which were stowed every requisite for a campaign upon the gold-fields.[238]

It is remarkable that despite this high level of equipage very few artifacts remain that can be positively identified as arriving with the gold seekers. While a surprising number of late 19th century Japanese coins are ascribed to Chinese gold seekers in regional museums, very few items carried or discarded by the way, as Woods describes, seems to have survived. An interesting exception would appear to be a small wooden cask in the procession of a local family in western Victoria. Family history describes this being given to a Great-great-grandfather, manager of a property near Edenhope, Victoria, close to the South Australian border - in exchange for food. What the cask may have contained is speculative: tea, dried fish, opium? That it had been consumed by the time the walker had spent perhaps three months on a ship before walking as far as the vicinity of Edenhope is likely.♦

Exoticism

Robe Customs House Museum in the absence of authentic artifacts has collected a number of 'Chinese' objects without much suggestion that any of these have anything to do with the actual walkers. These include a very new looking wicker basket described as 'antique Chinese', 'woven cane slippers' and a 'traditional pillow'. One object declared by it label to have been 'left by Chinese who landed in Guichen Bay' is an impossibly heavy and un-Chinese looking white marble mortar.

♦ See Image 7, p.47.

Image 11: Assorted "Chinese" objects, Robe Customs House Museum, assorted objects seen by author, April 2022.

As with the Japanese coins, any characters – Chinese or not – are likely to excite notice due to their exotic nature as far as largely monolingual English speakers are concerned. When Julian Woods remarked on how 'the bark of many a tree' was traced with Chinese characters he could only speculate on what they said. Many a later account have also been excited by such markings though they often exaggerate their distinctiveness by forgetting that the marking of trees in general was not uncommon at the time.[239] As Broadbent remarked in the journal of his trip to the goldfields: 'We passed a great number of inscriptions on trees, and left one as follows: "L. Broadbent's party passed here 21st February. All well."[240] Similarly Tolmer in the same year, 'Marked a tree, and left a note' at one point and at another 'indicated the spot by marking a gum tree with the words "Take to the left."'[241]

Behavior

One feature of the Chinese gold seekers remarked upon was their capacity to cook using a minimum of firewood: 'They display considerable ingenuity in availing themselves of the natural products of the country. A whole party will not use as much firewood as a single bullock-driver, and they will make a meal of food which would be rejected by the most hungry bushman.'♦[242] In general, however, there are

---

♦ A similar observation was made at Bathurst in NSW.

surprisingly few allusions to this large number of walkers passing stations and towns causing any disturbances apart from the novelty of the sight itself.

At Robe it was reported that 'the inhabitants suffered great inconvenience last year [1856] from their camping in the town', a problem solved simply by pointing 'out to each party, on landing, a suitable place to camp, a distance removed from the town'.[243] In March it was reported that 'up to the present time not a single complaint has been alleged against them on the part of the inhabitants of this township.'[244] In fact, the one clear contemporary negative comment stands out for its rarity. This is in a newspaper paragraph that exaggerates numbers – '5,000 landed last week at Guichen Bay' [perhaps 1,500 at most], before stating that: 'The roads are lined with parties of Chinamen, and the settlers are complaining of the depredations committed by them.'[245] If there were 'depredations' there seems to have been very little 'complaining' at the time.♦

There are also references to poor behaviour on the part of some Robe residents – 'manifold impositions practised upon

---

♦ Though this apparent restraint on the part of their ancestors did not stop such tales being repeated by later generations. See Part II below.

them by the land-sharks'. Though the generally good behaviour – even if these impositions caused them to have 'waxed somewhat indignant' – of the gold seeking arrivals from China seem to be endorsed by most observers.[246] One who witnessed the embarkation at Guichen Bay early in 1857 felt 'the Chinese are very kindly received by the inhabitants of all classes at Guichen Bay'.[247] While another, in reference to the regiment of soldiers sent to Robe, felt that 'as the Chinese were not long in moving off from Robe the unoccupied intervals became rather monotonous.'[248] Nevertheless, the 'terrible odds', calculated at '3000 to 100', should a 'general scrimmage' eventuate caused apprehension and was cited in the South Australian parliament as their own poll tax bill was being debated later that year.✽[249]

Overall, Henry Melville the Sub-Collector of Customs at the time felt the temporary arrivals from China were a benefit, 'for they paid for all they obtained, and must have left thousands of pounds in the district' even if 'on one occasion

---

✽ Though the passenger's lists would have a little over 1500 as the more likely number at the time this was said.

Ormerod's store was broken open by the Chinamen to obtain possession of the cases containing' opium.♥[250]

♥ The opium was confiscated for non-payment of duty, it being legal at that time.

(8) The natives rapidly disappearing – whose land?

The Robe walkers were doing so through land only recently usurped from its traditional owners, people who were still very much present in the landscape. The gold seekers arriving at Adelaide and Robe in 1856 and 1857 were entering the lands of such people as the Ngarrindjeri and Tanganekald on which a British colony had been imposed only some 20 years before. Despite this short period the colonies, through a mixture of introduced diseases and massacres, dominated both the indigenous peoples and the landscape to the extent that sheep and cattle were as plentiful as kangaroos and bandicoots, just more perilous for the native people to touch. These recent invaders were confident in their dominion, dividing up and selling the land to their own, and traversing the long distances with relative ease and a strong sense of entitlement to their passage free from attack or any hindrance by the former owners.

It was also only a little over ten years before the gold seekers from China began to walk from Adelaide to Victoria that 'the practicability of the overland route' from Melbourne to Adelaide had been established.[251] A journal account of a month-long trip in a 'tandem' from Port Philip to Adelaide in 1840 reported numerous sightings throughout of native people, their huts, dams and wells, and again in 1852.[252] Though within a few years of this the Governor of South Australia declared that: 'I have everywhere found the natives rapidly disappearing.'[253] Nonetheless, some ten years after the first Chinese walkers, native people were still reported in the area around the Coorong.[254]

These people of the Coorong would have been the Tanganekald and Ngarrindjeri people, numbering perhaps 3,000 at the time of the European invasion.[255] As the gold seekers walked further inland, they would have crossed the territory of the Bungandidj (Wattatonga) people. To the south around Hamilton were the Gunditjmara (Koroite), further north near Harrow the Jardiwadjali, and close to Ararat the Djab Wurrung. All these peoples would have been suffering the impacts of the recent invasions by British settlers through a combination of introduced diseases, land expropriation and massacres. In 1840 for example an incident known as the Maria massacre had resulted in two shootings and two hangings of Ngarrindjeri people.[256] While the Bungandidj around what is now called Mount Gambier were subject to the poisonings and other means of expropriation inflicted by the Henty's, who became wealthy (and respected) landowners as a result.[257]

Bonwick certainly saw native Australians on his travels, such as: 'Some half dozen Blacks were encamped opposite the Wickliffe Hotel.'[258] He also reported that: 'Ten years ago even the Koroite tribe mustered two hundred; there are now not one-fifth of that amount. There was a great fight upon Bryan's Creek in 1842, when forty-two Aborigines were slain.'[259] Apparently this did not destroy their resistance or perhaps Bonwick did not get the dates correct because in 1844 'the blacks drove off 400 sheep from the station of Mr. Cadden, of Bryan's Creek, speared several cattle of Mr. John M'Pherson, of the Glenelg, and so severely injured Mr. Wm. McEachern, his overseer, that his life is despaired of.'[260]

While direct contacts between the native peoples and the Chinese gold seekers are not well recorded Bonwick does make a direct comparison: 'I could not avoid contrasting the dark race of the past with the yellow faces thronging in upon us from the Flowery Land; a party of five hundred of the latter having camped the night before near Coleraine, cooking their rice in pans over fires laid in small holes scooped out of the ground.'[261]

These scattered post-invasion European observations of the Aboriginal communities take no account of the villages and houses that were part of the traditional lifestyle of for example the Gunditjmara people. The Aboriginal Protector George Robinson in 1841 described a village south of Hamilton as of 'thirteen large huts', 'warm and well-constructed', each in 'shape of a cupola or kraal'. This was a lifestyle that as the Chinese gold seekers passed through their lands had already been disrupted by pastoralists. With swamps and lakes later drained, and the re-use of stone walls, much evidence of their presence in the landscape has now been removed.[262]

While scanty there are a few recorded instances of interaction between local native people and the Chinese gold seekers. Woods reported a 'brisk business' that hints at one source of provisions: 'I could not help being amused by the business propensities of the blacks who were for the occasion doing a brisk business in magpies, jew lizards and native cats.[263] Such provisioning was not restricted to the Chinese walkers and Broadbent noted on his earlier trip that he 'bought from the blacks 38 fish for eight biscuits'[264]

Image 12: Eastern Quoll, aka Native Cat

While this was a peaceful interaction, Edward Hearne recalled hostility on part of native people local to Lake Wallace where he was running sheep:

> The blacks at Lake Wallace were much exercised at the sight of the Chinese. '"What name that fellow?" they would say. "Not a blackfellow; not a white fellow, only 'other fellow." The blacks, who were often good mimics, would place a stick with a bundle at the end of it across their shoulders and assume a jogging gait, in imitation of a Chinese jogging along with his load. They were disposed to be violent to the Chinese, but were restrained.[265]

(9) More than once was seen to shed tears
- hardship & self-help

While violence from first nation people was not one of the many hardships the walkers from the Pearl River Delta apparently had to endure.* Walking such distances, on good roads or bad, while carrying your belongings or supplies was undoubtedly a hardship no matter how used to walking as a basic means of transport people of the 19th century were. 'They carried their "swags" with poles as in China. Some of their loads weighed 2 cwt. [100 kilos] at least.'[266] Poor planning, loss of supplies or money, shipwreck, bad weather, disease, getting lost, etc, were always possibilities and are all recorded. With some 16,000 people verified as making this trek, that some if not many suffered hardship including death is unremarkable. That all or most suffered hardship, given the degree of planning and organisation recorded, not to mention the also numerous reports of good health, would seem unlikely. Though proportions are the one aspect the historical record consistently leaves uncertain.

---

* This is despite a rather dramatic account found in *The Poison of Polygamy*, an historical novel written a generation after the gold rushes by the son of a Chinese gold miner, Wong Shee Ping.

Hardship before arrival in Australia

While it is impossible to insure against all possibilities the organisational capabilities of the participants that conveyed so many thousands from the villages of the Pearl River Delta via Hong Kong to Adelaide and Robe achieved what they could. For example, faced with a voyage of three to four months, most shiploads of passengers seem to have brought their own doctor, such as Atong, or Yung Hing who stated he came 'as surgeon of the ship.'♣[267] We know of Yung Hing because of a dispute over landing but more often we only know about these medical practitioners when they proved unsatisfactory. The reaction when this occurred being rather spectacular on at least some occasions. Thus, even before arrival one ship captain 'discovered the doctor hanging in a slip knot by the neck, swinging near the cook's galley,'[268] Apparently a passenger had died of seasickness and his fellow passengers blamed the doctor rather harshly. In another case the doctor was 'bastinadoed'. Perhaps understandably as it was also reported that 'nearly half' the 'passengers are victims of disease.'[269]

♣ The length of the voyage was extremely variable. When the American clipper ship *Challenge* did the round trip between Hong Kong and Guichen Bay in 112 days it was considered an 'unprecedented short period.' While the *Young America* was 'only 37 days on the passage' from Hong Kong to Guichen Bay.

Atung appears to have been more fortunate as far as the attitude of his patients was concerned despite the fact that he seems to have had an especially diseased passenger list. Atung was the ships doctor on the *Manhow* which was shipwreck off Willunga. While all passengers landed, one named Jen-Song died, and this resulted in an autopsy and an investigation of the general health of all landed. After consultation between Atung and 'Dr. Jay, of Willunga,' it was found that not only did Jen-Song die of leprosy but that three others had this disease, while another had syphilis.[270] The level of disease on board the *Manhow* contrasts with that on a number of ships that arrived earlier that year of 1857. Arriving at Guichen Bay, these ships and their passengers were inspected by the 'newly-appointed Government Surgeon, Dr. Penny' who reported that the 'passengers were all perfectly free from disease.'[271]

Some ships certainly seem to have been less healthy than others with the 590 passengers of the *General Blanco*, '90 of whom were boys' suffering eight deaths, two of them suicides. While details are unknown, nineteen of the crew preferred 'three months with hard labour' to continuing to serve in this ship, or 'refusal of duty' despite inspections declaring the ship 'in a fit state to proceed to sea.'[272]

As perilous as the voyage itself might prove, getting off a ship could entail its own perils, especially if that ship was in danger of sinking. An eyewitness account of the landing of passengers off the *Phaeton* in early 1857, which soon afterwards sank, provides a glimpse of these perils in one dramatic instance:

> Sunday 1st: This morning between 8 & 9 saw a vessel very near the shore opposite the Township towards the long beach and to all appearance aground, Corpl Warren & P.Y. Ewens started immediately to the spot / about 5 or 6 pm? to give assistance if requested while there made her name out to be the "Phaeton" with Chinamen on board, during the day the yards were struck, and other nautical arrangements were made to try and save the ship, about 6 pm a boat came ashore followed by a raft loaded with 55 Chinamen. The line attached to the boat broke and the raft: The wind being S.W. drifted ashore in doing which the breakers extremely? high washed part of the Chinamen of the raft, but by the assistance of the Police and a boats crew they all landed safe. The remainder of the Chinamen were brought ashore in boats, The last of which came off at 10 PM, was informed that there was 10 feet of water in the ships hold waves were washing over her; and she was a total wreck, she had 260 Chinamen & about 700 tons of cargo, chiefly, Sugar, Tea, Butter, & oil, Captains name

Morrison, Corpl Warren & P.Y. Ewens returned to Station 11 P.M. having seen all the Chinamen landed. P.Y. Ewens returned to the wreck.[273]

Supplies

The prospect of starving on the walk depended on having sufficient supplies and such supplies could and were purchased in Adelaide. Robe however may not have been able to provide as much. Instead, what was able to be brought on the ship from Hong Kong may have been relied on, unless that ship was wrecked of course. In May 1857 the lack of a skilled harbour-master or reliable pilot at Guichen Bay 'where the presence of a number of reefs renders the navigation dangerous' was decried by an observer who claimed nautical experience.[274] At least three ships carrying Chinese gold seekers were wrecked in Guichen Bay during 1857 and although none of these passengers died as a result, they may not have been able to secure all their supplies. Certainly, the wreck of the *Phaeton* in February 1857 involved, one report tells us, 'The ruin of the Chinese passengers.' The writer knew this not from being in Robe but from Melbourne where he was able to observe:

that the Chinese portion, of the community in this city, on learning the particulars of the accident, have promptly subscribed and as promptly collected £500, and that they forwarded this sum per steamer *White Swan*, to the scene of the disaster, in charge of a trusty agent, to be disbursed in the most judicious manner, to meet the immediate wants of their ship-wrecked country men.[275]

It is not known if another 'large party of Chinamen' who later in the same year were 'thrown upon the Willunga coast by the stranding of the ship *Manhow*', also received help. According to an account by J. C. Howe who had been the local policeman, the group gathered seaweed, shellfish and even a dead shark washed on the beach to sustain themselves.[276] These ex-passengers numbered nearly 400 and some perhaps chartered the steamer *Burra Burra* while others walked, and by the time they reached the crossing of the Murray River at Wellington they had 'two drays to convey the sick and some baggage.'[277] Another wreck was the *Koenig Wilhelm II* whose 800 Chinese passengers also landed without loss, though in this case 16 crew drowned.[278]

Hardship after arrival

Shipboard illness and possible shipwreck were of course not the end of the dangers from disease and mishap, and it is concerning sick or injured people that the evidence is somewhat contradictory. There is ample evidence on the one hand of the sick or injured being cared for, carried on the drays, and otherwise supported by their companions. Nevertheless, there are also numerous accounts of apparently deserted people such as in Adelaide in 1856 when seemingly a man 'had been abandoned by his gold-seeking companions, who had started on their overland journey, without leaving him, either food or shelter.'[279] The following year part way to the goldfields another who had been ill for some time 'hanged himself from a tree' 'on the road to Cavendish lake'.[280] At Dunkeld, which is most of the way to the goldfields, it was reported that: 'when any of them become so unwell as to be unable to proceed towards his destination, his companions, without any scruples of conscience, abandon him to his fate.' In one case at least, 'George Gwyther, of the Woolpack Inn took him into his house' and 'opened a subscription list on his behalf, which was liberally supported.'[281]

All these examples come from the years 1856 to 1857 but another comes from the middle of 1858 and would appear to be of a man not only separated from his gold seeking companions but unable to continue his journey. This was more than half a year after the last ship full of Chinese gold seekers arrived at Robe and well after South Australia's own poll tax and tonnage limitation had been enacted.♦ In June 1858 a man known only as 'John Chinaman' was declared by 'Mr. R. B. Penny' surgeon of Robe town as 'of unsound mind' and 'destitute of means of support'. Or at least this is what the form asked and he was consequently 'to be conveyed to the Lunatic Asylum at Adelaide'. Curiously, once at the Adelaide Lunatic Asylum an apparent panel of at least four declared they were 'unable to find any symptoms of insanity in John Chinaman.' Had this man been abandoned by his companions and with no prospect of new arrivals to take him up did the local authorities at Robe seek to send him off elsewhere? The last we hear of John Chinaman – assuming it is the same person – is less than two weeks later when he is 'charged with throwing a quantity of hay on the roadway of King William-street'. Though reference to his 'son' and a confusion over horse feeding boys confuses the issue now as it did 'His Worship' then,

---

♦ See p.88 above.

who dismissed the case.[282] Whether he eventually completed his journey to the Victorian goldfields or was ever going there is unknown.

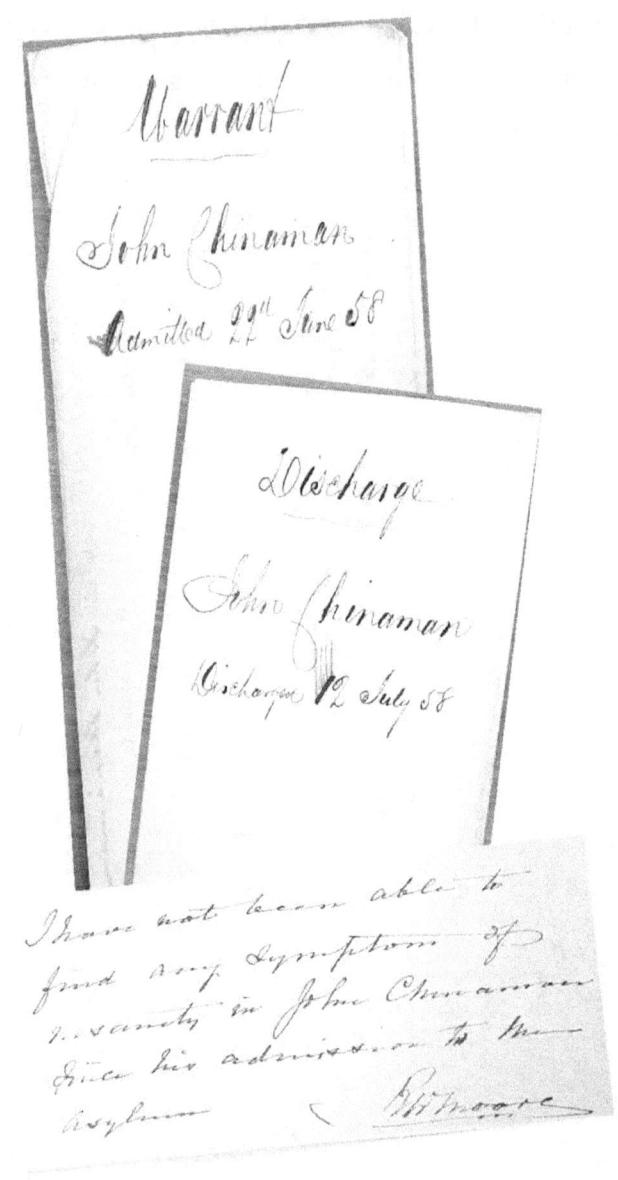

Image 13: Admission papers, Colonial Lunatic Asylum, 1858 unnumbered, John Chinaman, State Records SA: GRS 13461/00001.

The example of generosity by George Gwyther and his neighbours at Dunkeld contrasts with a rejection by the Adelaide destitute board, which declared that an application for admission to the hospital of a sick Chinese person 'could not be entertained'. This application was made not by the sick man's companions but by the shipping agents Younghusband and Co.[283] Soon after, this was clarified to allow admission as long as 'payment of a month's charges in advance' was made.[284] As a result, the following month several Chinese people suffering 'acute dropsy, the result of exposure to the inclemency of the weather' were in the hospital, as money was forthcoming from the 'treasurer of the party to which they belonged' who 'left his address, in order to facilitate the repayment of any further expenses'.[285]

Why some unfortunate gold seekers would be treated more harshly than others can only be speculated on. One possible explanation is that some individuals had no family or village companions willing or able to support them. While to Europeans all 'Chinese' at this period were the same, it was their family, dialect and district groupings which were the essential basis of organisation, business and self-help. In fact, the so called 'triads' or 'secret societies' often commented upon were in reality 'brotherhood' organisations designed to provide unconnected individuals just such support networks. The danger of not being so grouped being all too apparent in these cases of sickness and abandonment. Though another supposition is that those who left their fellow traveller under a 'hollow tree' in Adelaide did so knowing that the locals would take him to a hospital where it seems other similar 'pauper patients' were to be found.[286]

The importance of the distinction between people of the differing districts can be clearly seen in an episode observed by local landowner Edward Hearne♦ concerning one sick man left behind:

> Another party, when passing Lake Wallace North, left there a sick comrade who was unable to travel farther. He remained at the station for several months, during which time he partially recovered. As his health improved, he became anxious to proceed to Ballarat, and as he was still unable to go alone, he asked several troops of Chinese who passed to take him, but they would not. He was much chagrined at these refusals, and more than once was seen

---

♦ Published in 1920 by his grandson this account is based on the diaries of Edward Hearne. [The diaries themselves I have not been able to find.] Hearne was about 40 years old when an eyewitness to the Chinese gold seekers passing through western Victoria in the 1850s. Thanks to Andrew Latta for drawing my attention to this material.

to shed tears. When his host expressed surprise at the unwillingness of those who passed to help their less fortunate countryman the latter explained that they did not come from the same part of China as he. Eventually there came a party from his own district. The poor man was greatly excited by their advent, believing that now at length his prayer would be heard; that to the men of his own native province he would not appeal in vain. Nor was he disappointed, the newcomers agreed to take him. They placed him sitting or reclining in a large basket, which was suspended from a bamboo, each end of which rested on the shoulder of a Chinese, and so he was borne away.[287]

Hardship from the weather

Of course even those who did have support could nevertheless find themselves in danger from illness or, after a walk of hundreds of kilometres, at risk of simply being 'found dead on the way of hunger & thirst'.[288] Even successful arrival on the goldfields was no guarantee as with the 'about twenty-two' year old Ah Tong who 'was found dead in his tent', dying according to a *post mortem examination* of 'inflammation of the lungs, which the evidence went to show had been produced by cold and exposure during the late inclement weather'. The young Ah Tung having only arrived from Guichen Bay the day before his death.[289] That such deaths were the case for some is undoubted, though that it was a significant proportion of some 16,000 people who walked in search of gold is more difficult to say.

Certainly, cold weather, even when not walking was considered a cause of heightened mortality:

> The number of deaths which are occurring amongst the Chinese have induced many of them to leave the district, but the number daily arriving from Guichen Bay compensate for the departures. The number of Celestials at present in the district amount to about six thousand, and the number of deaths amongst them from the causes, from 1st July to 31st August, is eighty-seven. The greater part of these is "new chums," who have not become acclimated, and upon whom the severity of the winter is making sad havoc. The symptoms of this complaint, which is termed colonial fever, is somewhat similar to those exhibited by the Europeans, but the Celestials have also a painful swelling near the stomach and in the lower extremities. It is induced by cold and exposure, and a large number of those attacked are carried off by it. *Ovens and Murray Advertiser*.[290]

At the end of the winter of 1857 the Register reported 'the total number of deaths, including inquests, 177. Of this number no less than 53 were Chinamen, all but three of them being from Guichen Bay. The diseases of which they died are set down chiefly as those of dropsy and diseases of the lungs and heart.'♦[291] Assuming the Chinese segment of the population was less than one-third, this higher death rate was cause for concern. At least one medical practitioner in the goldfields thought so and 'Dr Allison then addressed a few words to the meeting, and discoursed upon the desirability of initiating the practice of giving Celestial lectures, and of paying every attention to their sanatory welfare. The Doctor's suggestions were interpreted and loudly applauded.'[292] Such lectures Dr Allison did indeed deliver:

> Dr Allison delivered his second lecture to the Chinese yesterday (Thursday) afternoon, at the encampment, Red Hill, to an audience of about one hundred. He impressed on them the necessity of preventing their countrymen landing at Guichen Bay during the winter months, and said they should only land here between November and

---

♦ Some were reported suffering from dropsy in Adelaide even before the walk. Dropsy: 'Pleural effusion occurs when fluid builds up in the space between the lung and the chest wall. This can happen for many different reasons, including pneumonia.'

June. They should also pay greater attention to the procuring of warm clothing, to personal cleanliness, to good tents, and a proper diet. The lecturer also explained the nature of the disease of water on the chest, from which so many of the Chinese have lately died, and at the conclusion received marks of approbation from his audience.[293]

By the end of 1857 it was considered that the death rates had risen and that 'a large proportion of the excess being Chinese, who have died from dropsy and diseases of the lungs, consequent upon the fatigues and privations endured by them in the overland journey from Guichen Bay, in South Australia'[294] People such as Ah Poo, Chow Nung and Ah Tin had spent months travelling from their villages by sea and land in the hopes of making money support or start a family only to die on the goldfields of Victoria.*[295]

Winter cold, the exhaustion of the long walk, coming straight after the long sea voyage, all no doubt compounded to weaken people's health. Regular inquests were held such as:

---

* Ah Poo from Guichen Bay died of dropsy after working for a time; Chow Nung a month later; Ah Tin, after 15 months, an addict. All seemingly winter arrivals.

On the body of a Chinaman, named You Kins, who had died suddenly on the forenoon of that day. From the evidence of a brother of deceased, it appeared that he had landed at Guichen Bay about two months ago, and had come over to Ballarat. He had not been complaining on the way. About four days ago he first complained of pains and a cough, and died about 11 o'clock this (Thursday) morning. Dr Mount stated that he had made a post-mortem examination, and considered the cause of death to be rupture of one or more of the cardiar vessels into the pericardium. Verdict accordingly.[296]

Many eyewitnesses attest to the exhaustion of the walkers. Such as Mr Snodgrass who declared he 'had been witness to a great deal of suffering upon the arrival of Chinamen on the gold-fields. Many of them reached the mines in a complete state of destitution.'[297] Later in 1862 similar accounts were that: 'They landed at Guichen Bay two or three weeks ago; and, what with the floods and rain that beset them on their journey, they have had a weary time of it.'[298] And: 'Several of them seemed foot-sore, and were very much travel-soiled; no doubt they will sleep soundly wherever they pass the night.'[299] Worse than foot-sore also: 'Our Smythesdale correspondent states that one of the Chinese recently arrived at that place from Guichen Bay, has died from exhaustion, through exposure and fatigue consequent on so long a journey. Dr Crossen was sent for on Thursday morning to attend the man, but on his arrival at China Town, life was extinct. An inquest will be held this day.'[300]

Nearly all of these accounts of increased death rates and death from exposure can be dated to the 1862 or 1863 arrivals which were late in the season. It was well known what the best walking season was: 'the early autumn is a far more convenient time for an overland journey than midwinter' before the winter rains when 'the roads over the large extent of low flat country hereabouts are in many places covered with water for miles, rendering travelling slow and tedious.'[301] That this seasonal window was taken into account most but not every time is apparent from the ships list of arrivals in Guichen Bay in 1857. Of the 31 ships listed, 28 arrived in the first half of the year, that is during the best walking season. A fact noted in Victoria when by October of 1857 it was reported that the 'Chinese Immigration, by way of Guichen Bay, has greatly fallen off.'[302]

Despite this a few ships did arrive later in the 1857 season and those that arrived in the brief 1862-63 period do not seem to have planned as well as their forerunners. It was noted that those off the *Buenavista* who arrived in August 'will find themselves on a very sublunary sphere now with this wintry weather' though the writer also thought 'they appear all hardy healthy fellows' who 'did not seem to take the slightest notice of the inclement weather'.[303] Though that description may not have been apt as by the end of a winter walk the new goldfields arrivals were described as 'poor fellows miserably clothed, and most of them barefooted, one by one entered the camp yard. One lad, aged about fourteen, was carried on the back; he looked wretchedly sick, and it is said the youth was thus carried for forty miles.'[304]

Resistance to hardships imposed

Hardship caused by disease, the weather or even lack of supplies on the journey was one thing, hardship caused by the actions of others another. Certainly, there were dark mutterings about the behaviour of people at Robe 'while the Chinese were passing through the port' that 'demanded as little should be known as possible, or our credit as fair-dealing [sic] Britons would certainly have been compromised.'[305] The 'breaking open the chests of the poor seamen' drowned off the *Koenig Wilhelm II* is suggestive of the morals of some in Robe at that time.[306]

Where poor behaviour occurred, there is also evidence of strong if not always effective resistance and complaints. Thus, when ordered to leave a ship at what they considered the wrong port the passengers 'armed to the teeth, resolutely maintained their position' against both crew and police efforts to evict them.[307] This was the case of the *Estrella do Norte*, a Portuguese ship out of Macao that had been chartered by a Hong Kong merchant to take its 242 Chinese passengers to Guichen Bay or failing that Adelaide and then arrange a passage to Guichen Bay by other means. These details the passengers well knew, hence the resistance when asked to leave the ship in Adelaide. The captain it seems had no intention of doing any more with his passengers and these passengers then appealed to the local law but were disappointed in the result.

Seeking local legal advice all 242 passengers at first sued Captain Goularte for the £3 cost of a fare to Guichen Bay. The magistrate however 'did not feel authorized in issuing the warrants applied for, but advised that a summons on behalf of one of the plaintiffs should be issued, which would have the effect of deciding the question of liability'.[308] This was done by Yung Hing who had travelled 'as surgeon of the ship' and asserted he had asked to be taken to Guichen Bay 'several times'. The defence then claimed that another passenger named Aku had 'acted on behalf of the others' and, apparently agreed that 'if they were repaid their money and rice [previously loaned to the Captain] then they would be content to leave the ship and go overland'. Despite the evidence of Affoo, who was also the interpreter, that he 'had come from Melbourne to look after the Chinese by the Estrella do Norte' and that he had 'asked Captain Cambridge, the sailing master of that vessel, to provide a passage for them to Guichen Bay' and 'no passage to Guichen Bay had yet been provided.' The Magistrate, to the surprise of the solicitor Mr Parker and journalists of both the *South Australian Register* and the *Adelaide Times* and no doubt the 242 Chinese gold seekers, found 'passengers by the Estrella do Norte might be considered as one family, and any agreement entered into by one would be binding on the whole.'[309]

Despite this failure to have their charterparty upheld legal remedies continued to be sought, at least by the merchants in Hong Kong whose experience of British justice in that colony was perhaps more positive. Thus, the recurring issue of being (over)charged when landing a Robe seems to have been long remembered. When arrival via Guichen Bay resumed after five years in 1862 a legalistic strategy, that must have been thought out in Hong Kong, was employed. This was to provide each passenger on the *Bonavista* with proof of their having prepaid any embarkation fee so that on arrival at Robe they 'held a copy of the agreement printed both in English and their own language'.[310] Unfortunately for the passengers once again the practical outcome of this appeal to law was not effective in the face of demands made on the ground. Though the fee to disembark was only 3s each compared to the 10s or more paid in 1857.[311]

In fact, resistance to being badly treated seems to have led to rumours of 'violent and threatening behaviour' 'to the bullock drivers and guides who bring them overland'. Though the observer of this rumour also felt on investigation that any 'ill feeling' 'invariably originated in the drunken habits' of the guides, 'and in their tendency to lose time at the various public houses' and so 'causing much loss' and 'nearly leading to some of them dying from starvation owing to their running short of food while coming through the forests'.[312] While Pon-Sa, mentioned above when arguing against the proposed residents tax, asserted that of those who landed at Guichen Bay many on the road 'died of hunger and thirst, and disease, and some hanged themselves.'[313] Not that these journeys were without hazards of other kinds such as when a 'bullock driver' employed as a guide 'drowned while bathing at Harrow in the Upper Glenelg' and his customers were 'left to find their way to Ballarat as well as they could'.[314]

On the goldfields

These hardships relate to the walk, though for many the real hardships began only after arrival on the goldfields where harassment including violent attacks and dispossession of claims was common. Foster the Chinese Protector spends more time remarking on relations – violent and non-violent – with non-Chinese miners than anything else in his journal.[315] In mid-1857, for example, there 'were about 6000 persons' at the Mount Ararat rush, 'one half of whom are Chinese. The Chinese were daily arriving overland from Adelaide.'[316] It was at Ararat it was acknowledged that 'it is to these adventurers [walkers from Guichen Bay] that we are indebted for the discovery of the lead which has caused the present rush'.[317] A 1990 memorial at Ararat makes the specific claim that Robe walkers off the *Francis P. Sage*

149

arrived in May 1857 to find gold and establish the town.[318] Despite this another observer reported: 'I believe many of the Chinese have had their 'claims' taken away forcibly; and there have been various propositions made by bodies of diggers to drive the whole of the Chinamen from the place.'[319] Even worse, that same month: 'The Chinese had possession of the best portion of the gold claims, and they were rushed by the miners, who also gave the unfortunate wretches a good thrashing and burnt their tents.'[320]

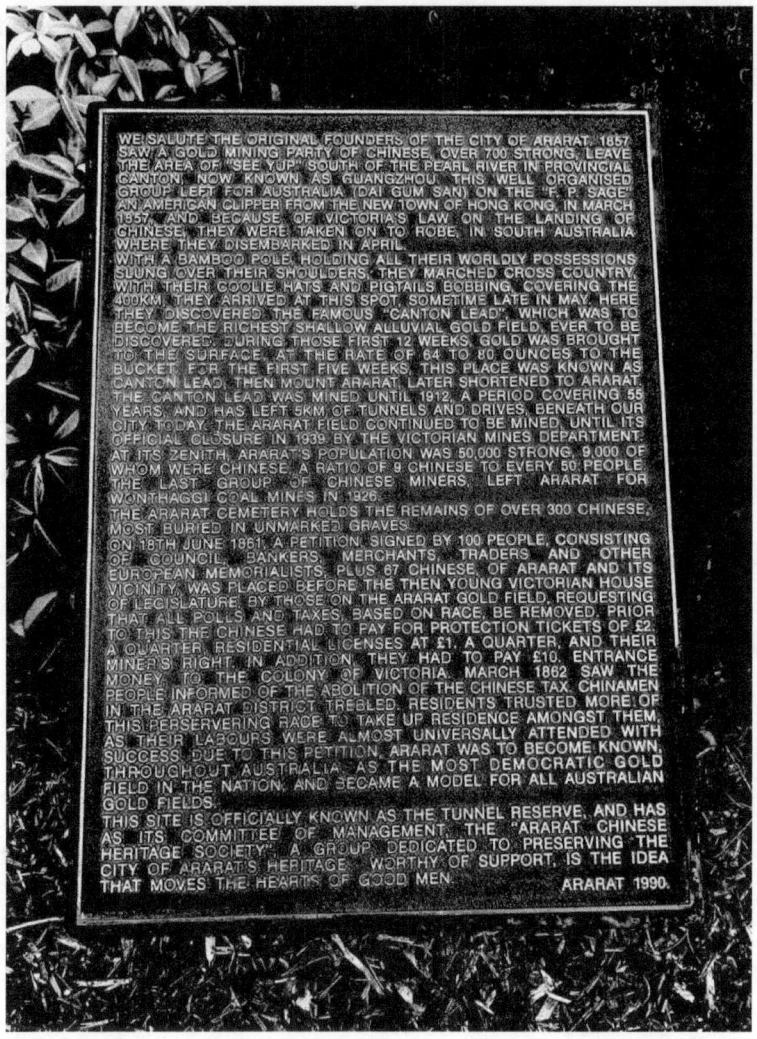

Image 14: Ararat Memorial, author photo, April 2022.

In addition to disputes over gold claims the Chinese shopkeepers were also subject to numerous brazen assaults and robberies, though legal redress in these cases was it seems more possible.[321] As well, the discovery of the rich Canton Lead by Chinese gold seekers and their continuing success, despite the hostility and being 'rushed' by some, seems to have led to an improvement in relations. It was reported a couple of months after the above incidents that, 'many an Englishman has joined the lucky Chinamen, and there is now a much better feeling existing between them'.[322] If this was the case it was short lived and by the following year a major jumping of claims was taking place, ostensibly enabled by a legal technicality generated by discriminatory licensing laws.[323]

Conclusion – A tough walk well organised

Thus far we can summarise the endeavour as a tough but well organised project. One that had perhaps more than its fair share of dodgy practices as ships captains tried to avoid their obligations. And of course, it cannot be forgotten that the whole was a diversion forced by the prejudices of the Victorian legislature. A prejudice that continued in various forms making the walkers lives hard even after arrival on the goldfields. However, in general it would appear that most of the treks were well-organised, well enough for some to recover from unforeseen disasters and/or to resist hardships imposed on occasion. Nevertheless, many undoubtedly died on the way or so exhausted themselves in the endeavour that their health was ruined with high death rates on the goldfields the noticeable result.

The bare bones of this trek to the goldfields have often been exaggerated or misinterpreted, much to the annoyance of fastidious historians. The chronology is plain enough but a broader context is needed to explain what was going on. A seemingly simple context can be seen in acknowledging that walking long distances was not unusual. From this the basic motivations of the people involved, the racism that they encountered and the organisation they already had in place helps to explain the reaction to the poll tax. From this the organisation of the alternative routes to the goldfields can be understood, including capacity to handle deceptions and find alternative routes such as via Robe. The Victorian reaction and the difference with the later group's needs be understood before examining overall costs and the details of the trek itself. Within the colonial context the overall hardship and reactions to various impositions can be better understood.

Part II

(10) Wells, walls and woolsheds – folklore & myths

While the image of the Robe walks as a 'long march' ordeal imposed by devious ships captains can be strongly rejected. This still leaves a surprising number of myths associated with the walkers that continue to exist, at least among the locals of western Victoria, if not in the Australian population generally. The journey from Robe, which entailed a significant number of people, was a well-organized and widely recognized undertaking that successfully hindered the efforts of Victoria's legislators. Despite this, a multitude of myths and stereotypes have been associated with this historical event, which surpass the typical dramatizations and simplifications that are characteristic of all historical accounts. These myths can be classified into three categories: those related to the landing at Guichen Bay, those pertaining to the circumstances surrounding the journey, and those attributing certain activities to the walkers.

The first two categories can be partially explained by a desire for sensationalism and a tendency to portray the participants as victims of oppression and inferiority. These inclinations have resulted in the selective presentation of incidents and exaggerated generalizations derived from them. Although instances of hardship and mistreatment did occur, they do not appear to have been representative of the journey as a whole, particularly given the number of participants involved. In reality, such incidents seem to have been relatively infrequent. The third category is characterized by the attribution of numerous infrastructure projects in western Victoria to Chinese origin, a phenomenon that appears to be rooted in an excessive fascination with the exotic.

The root of this exoticism – apart from the obvious racism and eurocentrism – is the whitewashing of Australian history that was an adjunct to the White Australia policy. The result of which is that Chinese people as victims and either gold seekers or market gardeners is all that many people know or can conceive of Chinese Australian history. Chinese opera performances, the building of temples, the many stores and shops, intermarriage and families established, the many Chinese doctors, the businesses founded, the links with Hong Kong, the importance of Christianity, bones return, self-help societies, and international banking, are all usually left out of account. What this means is that in the absence of a wider context implausible explanations more easily take root and through sheer repetition take on a life of their own.

Myths associated with the landing at Guichen Bay

The first group of myths are clustered around the actual landing at Guichen Bay. The most noteworthy aspect of which is that these nearly always neglect the arrival of thousands of gold seekers from China throughout 1856 who either landed at Adelaide to proceed directly to the goldfields or who took a coastal steamer to Robe in order to shorten their walk. This 'forgetting' of aspects of the history then allows for some significant distortions. The greatest distortion being that the Robe arrival of the *Land o' Cakes* and the subsequent numbers in 1857 were a 'surprise' and even more hysterically an 'invasion' in some sense. The sense of suddenness and lack of control is further heightened by the emphasis placed on either the ships captains determining the destination or the landings themselves being harsh in various ways.♦[324]

♦ Sprengel, *Robe's Chinese invasion*, is strongest in asserting a Captain 'decided to give Victoria a miss', being ignorant both of charterparties and the route via Perth that meant Adelaide (and Robe) came before Victoria.

The lack of context for the 1857 arrivals direct from Hong Kong and the fact that Robe residents took this increase in numbers in their stride at the time has been discussed above.♣ Once this broader context for the 1857 arrival of the larger ships is acknowledged then much of the dramatic element so loved of Robe based local historians and others is transformed. It remains a dramatic and interesting history of course, just not a surprise invasion of people thrown on a barren shore and forced to march ill-equipped into an unknown land.

Captains' choice
The other element often forgotten is the nature of transport between the Australian colonies and places like Hong Kong. At the period of the walk captains and ship owners (sometimes the same person) would enter into an agreement with a trader or group of passengers known as a charterparty. Legally enforceable and taken seriously, we have seen a number of court cases demonstrating that while some captains did mislead their passengers and break their charterparties this was by no means the usual circumstance.♥ In other words, if hundreds of passengers at a time from the

---

♣ See p.80 above.
♥ See pp.55-57 above.

villages of south China landed in Guichen Bay this was because that was where they were intended to land.

Thus, when Cawthorne described the captain of the *Land o' Cakes* as 'purposely' missing Victoria she was ignorant both of his route – via Perth and thence Guichen Bay before ever reaching Port Philip – and that he was contracted by Hong Kong based merchants to do precisely what he did.[325] Horsfall also saw the skippers as 'canny' in their role of having 'discovered' Robe despite its extensive use the previous year as the embarkation point for hundreds of Chinese walkers coming down from Adelaide.[326] Nevertheless, we have also seen that some captains did attempt to break their agreements and these cases – more widely reported – may have been the origin of the impression that it was the ship captains who were determining destinations.

Landing costs

Adelaide was the favoured port for ships from Hong Kong all through 1856, even though many gold seekers subsequently took coastal shipping down to Robe to shorten their walk. As such there are no reports of difficulties with landing at either place. Not at Adelaide presumably because as a main port the landing of passengers was routine and well serviced. While at Robe the smaller coaster steamers could come in closer to Guichen Bay where the relatively new jetty was described at the beginning of 1856 as a 'convenient Jetty, with a tramway from the road to the end, is now completed, having at its extremity six feet at low water.'[327] The smaller steamers could also only carry a limited number of passengers – low hundreds at most – that presumably did not overwhelm the local capacity to land them. It was only in 1857 that Robe became the favoured port for larger ships direct from Hong Kong and it is only under these changed circumstances that accounts of ill-treatment, overcharging and drowning arise.

Image 15: Robe Town from original sketches by A. Tolmer, c.1850s, SLNSW DSM/Q983.8/T

As with devious captains, it is not a question of ill-treatment, or overcharging and drowning not occurring, but whether these conditions were common, frequent or typical. Guichen Bay did not allow the larger vessels out of Hong Kong to approach the shore as closely as they might at Port Adelaide or as could the smaller coastal ships. This meant that the boats taking passengers off the larger vessels needed to travel much further out than with the screw steamers they were used to working with which could come in closer to shore or even allow use of the jetty. The boatswains who charged 10/- to carry people off these unaccustomed Hong Kong vessels into Robe no doubt felt a great deal more effort and risk was entailed. While many observers felt this was good money, given the strain on resources and the opportunity for ready payment in cash, it was not perhaps unreasonable.♦328

Calculations of costs in the past that are meaningful today are difficult and certainly we have seen that the Chinese passengers themselves often thought the fare for landing excessive and on occasions protested. But this is perhaps

---

♦ Apparently, the pilots at Guichen Bay also charged more than the ship captains thought reasonable with '16s. a foot is too much for bringing a ship up to an anchorage'.

partly because any cost at all was thought excessive, with apparently many believing landing was part of the fare already paid. Within the general perception of the Chinese gold seekers as rather hapless victims of nearly everyone they came in contact with, the idea that the Robe boatswains gouged them mercilessly is plausible and numerous accounts have presented it that way. Eric Rolls for example asserted: 'They paid extortionate sums to get to land.'[329] However, when the careful organisation that seems to have characterised much of the effort to get people from their villages to the goldfields is considered, along with the many instances of both physical resistance and appeals to law, the idea of meek acceptance of excessive price gouging becomes less so. In fact, it is the very protests at these charges – reasonable, high or excessive as they may have been – that seems to have inspired the exaggeration of the imposition in later accounts.

Landing dangers

Regardless of cost, passengers needed to be landed and this procedure could have its own dangers. The relative safety of Guichen Bay for shipping was somewhat contested. The Port Adelaide Harbour Master gave it high marks for safety when he inspected it in 1855. In detailed instructions for shipping

161

Bloomfield Douglas commented 'that it is undoubtedly a most valuable anchorage and harbour of refuge, …'[330] Yet, this report is full of mention of reefs and references to rocky points that need to be 'carefully avoided'. Perhaps Bloomfield Douglas did not envisage Guichen Bay becoming a regular drop off point and so his standard for a 'refuge' was much lower.

The accounts of vessels that foundered in this 'valuable anchorage' in 1857 would seem to throw doubt on this report and it would also appear that the various captains of these larger ships were justified if they were anxious to off load their passengers as quickly as possible. As Henry Melville the Harbour Master at Guichen Bay throughout 1857 explained:

> Masters of course were anxious to get cleared as soon as possible many of them not being prepared to ride out a gale their chains never having been out of the lockers and in some cases vessels had not sufficient length of cable it required one hundred and twenty fathoms to ride out a gale with security, I often worked night and day to get these ships out of Harbor and was as pleased to see their fore top sails in the offing as the captains themselves.[331]

Between anxious captains, changeable weather, and the need to transfer passengers and their luggage into small boats, there would seem ample scope for poor behaviour and difficulties, including drowning. Certainly, these aspects have been emphasised in the accounts.♦³³² A difficulty in assessing the hardship and dangers of landing at Guichen Bay that these accounts allude to is how to evaluate the evidence of death or hardship? As with the court accounts of captains evading their agreements, are such reports typical and illustrative or are they exceptions that have found their way into the historical record precisely because they are exceptional or at least more dramatic than the usual? To answer such a question a record of both the exceptional and the mundane would be required, something newspapers by their nature rarely provide outside such things as shipping reports. Fortunately, in the case of the Robe landings of 1857 this is exactly what we do have.

For the years 1856 and 1857 we have both the daily journal of the police stationed at Robe and the private journal of one of those police. In both are recorded their mundane activities

---

♦ Sprengel, *Robe's Chinese invasion*, for example, says 15 Chinese men died at Guichen Bay but as this is the number of the crew drown with the wreck of the *Koenig William,* he no doubt confused these.

including the many times one or more of the Robe police oversaw the landings of the Chinese gold seekers.[333] The journals are tersely written and give the impression of much watching and only intervening when necessary, though one entry does report 'Corp Warren and Private Ewens assisting Sub-Collector in examining the luggage of 265 Chinamen landed from the ship "Land o Cakes".'[334] Private Ewens in his personal journal records Chinese men arriving by various steamers and schooners at Guichen Bay in 1856 but only reports one incident. This was when 'a Boat load of Chinamen capsized'.✦ He and another trooper subsequently hunted among the rocks and along the beach 'for Chinamens goods'.[335]

From the Guichen Bay Police Station Records it can be seen that of the 33 ships in 1857 arriving direct from Hong Kong only six are recorded as associated with an incident worthy of record by the police.♣ Of these six, three are ships – the *Phaeton, Sultana, Koenig William II* – that were wrecked off Guichen Bay. In each of these three wrecks all the Chinese passengers were landed without any fatalities.[336] In the case

---

✦ The spelling in the journal is patchy and is preserved here.
♣ The Guichen Bay Police Station Records do not mention the arrival of 10 ships that are recorded in the Customs list, but does record two coastal steamers that are not on this list.

of the *Phaeton* and the *William Miles* some Chinese passengers were thrown in the water before reaching the beach or jetty.[337] Soon after the arrival of the *William Miles* the body of 'a Chinaman was lying dead', though no cause of death was determined or even if he was actually from the *William Miles*.[338] The arrival of the *Pudsey Dawson* saw the drowning of one passenger when the landing boat capsized.[339] Finally, the *Salsette* saw a dispute over landing fees recorded.[340]

Image 16: Title page, Guichen Bay Police Station Records, State Records SA: GRG5/159, 1851 – 1863

Thus, in a year when over 16,000 Chinese gold seekers landed at Robe the evidence of the police at the spot is that two deaths were reported, at least twice people were in the water, three times ships were wrecked, though without loss of the life of any passengers, and once a dispute reached sufficient tempo to come to the attention of the police. While no doubt much escaped the notice of the police this is not the record of an inherently dangerous situation or one noteworthy for anything other than the large numbers that must have been in and around Robe at any one time. Remarkably the police do not seem to have been involved in any incident involving the Chinese gold seekers in Robe once they had landed.

Despite the low-key police reporting there are numerous contemporary reports that show greater concern for the ill-treatment Chinese passengers received. This includes by the Governor of South Australia, though none report any deaths or incidents not found in the police journal. Father Julian Woods, for example, was also an eyewitness and he spent some time re-telling his stories at fundraisers and such like in after years. These accounts, told in an 'entertaining style' some 20 years later, may have led to his version gaining greater notoriety. According to Woods:

> A large amount of money was made by bringing them ashore in boats for the captains of the various vessels used to decline in most cases to do more than bring them to the anchorage.

These and other indignities such as threatening to pitch them overboard when they would not go ashore at the moderate rate of 5/- led to an outbreak on one occasion.[341]

Not long after Woods passed through Robe, an instance of 'brutal acts of violence' that did involve being pitched overboard was recorded, though the context was the almost immediate arrest of the four crewmen considered responsible by the sole police officer then at Robe.[342] According to the police journal:

Wedy... 18th
William Miles arrived with 700 Chinamen, & as the Capt. commenced landing Chinamen at night Corpl... Warren thought it proper some policemen should be on the jetty, accordingly went on duty and servicemen up all night. Between the hours of 2 & 3 A.M. one of the boats instead of landing the Chinamen on the jetty, the crew threw over some of them before reaching it on seeing which Corpl... Warren took the boats crew in charge consisting of 4 men, on the way to the station one man bolted (Scotti) after locking the other three up search was made for Scotti heard he had gone on board his ship.
Thusy... 19th

Corpl... Warren apprehended the man Scotty and brought the prisoners before C.P. Brewer Esq S.M. 3 of the crew were fined £5 (including Costs) and the other was discharged.[343]

A couple of days later it was reported 'that a Chinaman was lying dead on the roadside about ten miles on the road to the "Stone Hut".' As there was no evidence of a struggle the man's death was considered "natural" and he was buried on the spot by Private Wren, who also found 'one schilling in a purse tied round the wrist of the corpse'.[344] The casual burial in this March case is in contrast to the drowning of another man in May that same year. This resulted in a jury being sworn 'to hold an inquest on the body at the Robe Hotel'. 'Two of the jurors were fined 20/- each for nonattendance' and both 'Capt. Harrison of the ship Pudsey Dawson and Septimus McKenzie Licenced waterman' gave evidence. 'The jury brought in a verdict of accidental death by drowning.'[345] The next day 'Corp. Warren employed three "Blacks" to dig the grave & bury the body of the Chinaman, for doing which Corp. Warren paid them 10/1.'♦[346]

♦ Corp Warren invoiced the Destitute Board for this cost.

Thus, there were undoubtedly circumstances of violence and ill-treatment that occurred at Robe, even at least two deaths. Yet, within the context of a well-planned movement of numerous people over a year these are not circumstances that can be said to characterize the movement as a whole. Eric Rolls in citing this incident implies that it was just one example of many and so is being misleading in his search for drama.[347] He is by no means the only one.

The false belief that many Chinese landing at Guichen Bay were in such poor condition that they required assistance in turn made plausible another myth that is commonly repeated. This is that the wife of the local magistrate, Elenore Mary Brewer died of typhoid as a result of caring for Chinese suffering this disease. Cawthorne, Sprengel and Rolls all repeat this myth.♣[348] Her death in March 1856 was in fact when the only Chinese arrivals were by steamer from Adelaide where if suffering typhoid they would not have been allowed to proceed. In fact, it would appear more likely that Mrs Brewer died as a result of caring for a group of 'Highland immigrants' who arrived suffering 'sickness' – typhoid is never mentioned. Though a report to the Female

---

♣ Perhaps following family lore as John Brewer also repeats this, or at least his transcriber John Cantrell.

Immigrant Board concerning the cancellation of rations to these same immigrants by C. P. Brewer, mentioned in the same month his wife died, contains no hint of any association between the two.[349] In popular folk memory however the impoverishment of many immigrants from Scotland is forgotten while the image (largely false) of Chinese arrivals as victims persists.

Myths relating to the circumstances of the walk

In reality, as many contemporary accounts demonstrate, the arrival of gold seekers from southern China created no major problems in Robe itself and, despite their large numbers, they set off quickly on their long walk. Nevertheless, the circumstances of the walk itself are also often characterised in terms of great hardship even death by starvation as well as ill-treatment such as abandonment by their guides. As with the landings at Robe, it is not that harsh incidents involving ill-treatment or even death did not occur, but that very often a single incident is reiterated as an (assumed) example of a general state of affairs for which there is no evidence. Accounts such as those found in the Victoria Collections or in a popular author such Eric Rolls are cherry picked – not intentionally perhaps – as instances of starting with a fixed idea or unquestioned assumption and just as unquestioningly "finding" the evidence to support it.♦ These are accounts that are possibly true in specific circumstances and are undoubtedly dramatic in the retelling – in fact that is why they made the news in the first place – but all too easily slip from being untypical into being perceived as typical.

Exhaustion & starvation

A common element of the story is that exhaustion and even starvation on the journey was common. As one petition by those who had actually walked the route described it: 'We feel it hard, ... to have to come overland, and many in hunger, others sick, and some die.'[350] While this petition was trying to generate sympathy to prevent yet another tax being levied on Chinese goldminers, that there was hunger, sickness and some deaths is undeniable. Yet we have seen that the movement was too well planned for this to have been an unvarying or even regular occurrence. It has even been seen that when unforeseen disasters did strike, as with a deceitful captain or a shipwreck, resources could be applied for to assist that were readily forthcoming.♣ Nevertheless, it was a long walk and some walkers undoubtedly did arrive

---

♦ For these examples from the Victorian Collections and Eric Rolls see p.173 and p.169.
♣ See p.132.

exhausted and some no doubt died on the way. As another eyewitness described: 'All the day following I kept passing small struggling parties upon whom fatigue was doing heavy execution. Some had already knocked up and were being carried upon bamboos. They seemed kind and attentive to each other ...'[351]

However, there is little evidence that extreme exhaustion or starvation was a typical or even a common outcome. In fact, the one piece of evidence from the Chinese Protector W. H. Foster based at Ballarat that is sometimes used to prove frequent hardship and starvation actually demonstrates the opposite.[352] As with the police journal at Robe the Chinese Protectors letter book runs over the period under question - from 1855 to 1859 - and in his account Foster continuously comments on the 'Chinese population'. Foster in only one brief period comments that: 'Great mortality prevails at the various Chinese encampments arising principally I am informed from the hardships and privations of the overland journey from the Adelaide District and the want of proper accommodation for the sick upon their arrival at this place.' Within a week he is reporting that: 'Mortality among the Chinese has been on the decrease since my last report.'[353] In all other periods he comments only about their arrival, the lack of taxes they pay by taking this route or the (often violent) relations between the Chinese and non-Chinese miners. The dates as to why the Chinese Protector is suddenly concerned with the health of the arriving walkers gives us a clue as to what is happening. Nearly all the ships arriving at Guichen Bay in 1857 do so in the first half of the year. Only three do so in the second half, one in November and two in August. Foster must be referring to walkers off one or perhaps both of these August ships who, arriving late in the season, walked in far wetter weather than those who arrived earlier. The sudden arrival of a group in very poor health causes Foster great anxiety just because it is an unusual occurrence. To use his account to demonstrate that such poor health was a typical outcome of the walk is a case of taking evidence out of context.♦

Provisions & Cash

Considerations of exhaustion and starvation raises questions of what provisions were carried or could be obtained on the way. As mentioned previously we are unsure of what

---

♦ As does for example Kathryn Cronin, *Colonial casualties: Chinese in early Victoria*, Melbourne University Press, Melbourne, 1982, p.49 and the Victorian Collections, *The Treks from Robe* by Cash Brown, https://victoriancollections.net.au/media/exhibitions/5fbd874fd5fa8108 043fc293//5fc8d9e89992142684f04d6a/original.pdf.

provisions the Chinese gold seekers brought with them or how they obtained provisions on the way. We do know they were often well prepared and had cash money for purchasing, sometimes obtained by selling goods brought with them. This they could do at sheep stations along the way or even from local indigenous people. This is a rather excitable account of provisioning from the later walkers of 1862:

John Chinaman Overthrown. — A number of celestials came to a sheep station the other day seeking "sheepy". I ordered a shepherd to bring in a mixed lot of ewes and wethers, with a few huge toothless Leicester rams amongst them. The eyes of the celestials at once fastened on the old rams, and, pointing to one of them, the interpreter asked "How much?" "Sixteen shillings," I replied, and he at once handed over the money. They seized the poor ram, and with a piece of cord fastened it by the horns to the centre of their carrying pole. When they essayed to march, however, the ram, with his fore feet propped out, refused to move. Hereupon they spoke to each other in their own language, when one came up and gave the ram a poke behind which caused it to leap head fore-most on the seat of honour of the Chinaman, and send him sprawling in the dirt. Away went the ram at full speed, dragging the long bamboo with him; and away went three hundred "soapy faces" after it, all shouting and yabbering together, with a din that would have caused the dons of Babel to "shut up."— Cor.[354]

Father Woods also provides us with tantalising observation, this time from the first walkers: 'The celestials unfortunately showed too great an anxiety in their bargaining in consequence of which native cats sometimes were quoted at 9d.'[355] Another eyewitness, Edward Hearne reported that: 'They asked eagerly for "licee. licee," but it may be imagined that such numbers soon exhausted the supplies of rice in the district, and the latter troops had to content themselves with meat and wheat, which latter they boiled, it may be feared, somewhat imperfectly.'[356] The published excerpts from the diary of Hearne goes on to say: 'They appeared to be amply provided with money, and paid readily for whatever they got. Edward Hearne had a pile of sovereigns, bank notes, and silver coins, including Spanish dollars, that the Chinese paid him for supplies of food. This money he disposed of by distributing it among his labourers in payment of their wages.'[357] James Bonwick implies the walkers were well cashed up when he reported: 'These Overlanders from Guichen Bay are regarded with great benignity by our western store-keepers.'[358]

Guides

Woods also observed the dangers of the bush for everyone, including 'the great frequency of persons being lost in the bush'[359] This was something the Chinese gold seekers were perfectly aware of and the hiring of guides or at least dray drivers was observed from their first arrival at Adelaide and from Robe also.♦ Later accounts often retell stories of guides abandoning walkers, sometimes only a short way along the track, though no contemporary evidence of this can be found. There are however numerous contemporary reports that do mention these guides. Apart from those that praise the guides we have accounts of guides being drunk and wasting time, along with the fact that the Chinese walkers did not put up with such behaviour.♣ Another report is an obvious misunderstanding of the Glen Osmond dispute referred to above: 'We are informed-though we cannot vouch for the truth of the assertion-that considerable danger is attached to the duties.' In this confused account it is not the Chinese treasurer who is nearly killed but a guide that is accused of the theft. The journalist seems to have felt some doubt about his informers as he ended the account: 'The story is a strange one if true.'[360]

♦ See pp.105-106 above & Guichen Bay Police, 11 June 1856.
♣ See p.148 above.

That such guides or draymen might not be too scrupulous in general is evident: 'There have been several dray-men selling goods and spirits on the way, and two of our merchants have lost by the drunkenness and villany of some Geelong draymen to the tune of several hundred pounds. The men are still at large.'[361] While usually referred to as "guides" the men hired by the Chinese walkers might merely have been drivers, for Edward Hearne reported: 'They were generally under the guidance of some of their country men, who, having previously lived in, and gained a knowledge of Australia, had gone home to bring back bands of their fellows under contract to work together on the goldfields. The leader was usually mounted, though poorly, but his numerous followers were on foot, each man having a bamboo across his shoulder with a basket at either end.'[362] This leadership may have varied with the group, and in 1862 it was thought that: 'This Celestial addition to our population was on its way direct from Guichen Bay, and had a white man for leader.'[363]

Myths relating to activities supposedly undertaken by the walkers

Exaggerated or untypical as these accounts of ill-treatment and starvation would appear to be, they at least are plausible within the historical context. Of quite another level of myth are the many stories that apparently to still circulate in the regions and towns along the routes taken by the Chinese gold seekers. Usually concerning infrastructure projects, these accounts would have us believe that a rather startling range of constructions, ranging from wells to woolsheds to extensive stone walls, can be attributed to the Chinese walkers.[364] In all cases there are no contemporary collaboration of these stories, with their first appearance being at the earliest some 40 years after the events. In many cases the dates cannot be made to coincide with the years when the walkers were walking, a narrow range after all, either 1856-1857 or 1862-1863. And in nearly all cases there are perfectly clear alternative explanations for the structures that do not require the employment of men anxious to get to the goldfields and unskilled in that kind of work.

That employment in building these structures is implausible is clear from the accounts given above. The men from south China were well organised and indebted for the specific purpose of reaching the goldfields to pay off said debts and to begin earning money for their families in China. The idea that they would stop for any length of time to earn what would only have been a smaller income makes no sense. Of course, as we have seen, many of the writers dramatizing the walk were not familiar with details such as the organisation or indebtedness of the gold seekers. Instead, these writers are perhaps imagining a rather hapless, impoverished group of starving stragglers for which such work would be welcome or essential. Where some feel even this motivation is insufficient, even more implausible explanations are alluded to. Such explanations include not just a need to earn money or provisions, but to avoid being denounced and subject to arrest (for what was not in fact against the law), even being held captive. Another common suggestion is that the work was done by people returning to an area with which they were familiar within a few years after passing through. This last explanation however involves a conflation with Chinese workers of another generation entirely.

Chinamen's Well

One of the most common of the myths that seems to pervade the entire route is that the walkers continuously dug wells or even that they are responsible for all the remaining wells in the region. This myth seems to be partly based on the assumption that the Chinese gold seekers were walking through virgin territory.*³⁶⁵ A European survey party passing down the Coorong years before the walk began in 1844 found numerous wells: 'At about 5 miles [beyond Salt Creek] we came to a well of water, ... the well contains the best water for many miles ...'³⁶⁶ Some were native wells but many seem to have been dug by the various travellers and others: 'The whalers had a station (two huts) on shore, and had dug a well, in which there was good water.'³⁶⁷ On occasions the survey party themselves 'dug a well with water within a foot of the surface'.³⁶⁸

Tolmer in 1852 reported that a 'native says, water could be obtained by digging'. A day after he crossed the Murray and heading south east Tolmer stated that he 'saw some native signal-fires to the N.E.' Camping, he found that 'here two or three wells have been sunk'. Though Tolmer himself used 'water-kegs' and had 'a pack-horse to carry water'.³⁶⁹ Not only were their numerous native water holes but numerous South Australians and non-Chinese gold seekers had walked these routes and of course used or dug numerous wells, including some wells established by government paid

---

* In fact, the first Adelaide to Port Philip overland trip was in 1841.

sappers.[370] Water was as we saw plentiful for most of the route and in fact too much water was often the problem.[*]

The first segment of the walk from Robe to Penola was describe at the beginning of 1856 as 'very sandy and through an uninteresting description of country, wooded with very small trees', though there were places 'where swans, ducks, and turkeys abound'. The reputedly first European overland walkers in 1841 described the land as 'watered by immense swamps of fresh water, which we found very difficult to cross.'[371] In fact, the stretch along the Coorong has quite a number of wells: 'Such sites include Chinamans Well, Sheoak, Salt Creek, Woods Well, Cantara and Coolatoo and Coconut Well.' 'Both on the peninsula and along the inland side of the Coorong, there are many waterholes marked on old hundred maps.'[372] Not that the need for water or wells was non-existent or always easy. Speaking of the Coorong in 1856, for example, it was reported that: 'Numerous wells have been sunk with one result—salt, salt, salt.'[373]

All of which is not to say that the Chinese walkers did not dig their own wells – given the large numbers in their groups this is in fact probable – but there is nothing to suggest which

---

[*] See p.71, p.92 and p.144 above.

181

ones nor that any of those that remain today are in any recognisable 'Chinese' style. Yet many wells are named Chinaman or Chinamans Well, perhaps due to association with a market gardener of a later generation. Even more remarkable are the many stone or brick cisterns – which are for water storage and not wells at all – which are also attributed to Chinese.♦³⁷⁴ This is an attribution seemingly on the basis that these once common pre-galvanised tank structures of very English design are now as unfamiliar as the Chinese gold seekers.♣

♦ 'Underground tanks were a typical component of nineteenth century rural properties in Victoria, …'
♣ Three times while tracing the walk – at Robe, Harrow, and Dunkeld – were "wells" said to have been built by Chinese, all were cisterns. Author's personal communications, April 2022.

Image 17: Dunkeld Cistern, author photo, April 2022.

Remarkably not only do these stories concerning various wells and even cisterns of an obviously much later date persist but one well in particular – Chinamen's Well on the Coorong – has achieved a remarkable status as a fake tourist site. The well is known as Chinamen's Well and is near Salt Creek on the Coorong. The well is of a unique design and the lack of evidence for who built it or even exactly when and why in this unusual style only adds to the mystery. This is a mystery the attribution to the Chinese walkers seems to resolve, as long as the Chinese walkers themselves are also seen as mysterious. In this instance Chinamen's Well even has an 'official' (i.e. government paid for) tourist sign declaring the well to have been built by Chinese people despite the lack of any evidence for this beyond its name, and with any plausibility for this being non-existent. This appears to be a good example of the "name inspires a story which justifies the name" circularity of myth making.

Image 18: Chinaman's Well today, author photo, April 2022.

Before discussing the builders of this particular well it is worth noting that: 'The only evidence of habitation is a small Aboriginal cockle (Donax) midden 14 cm below surface which is suspected to be 2- 4000 years old.'[375] It is only in the 19th century that a well on the Coorong early acquired the name Chinaman's Well or even Chinaman's Wells. This is a designation so casually mentioned by government surveyor Todd – 'at a place called the Chinaman's Wells' – that if it was more than an ordinary well at that time it would seem to be of long standing rather than new built. Newly built being what it would have had to have been if built for and by the walkers in 1856.[376] Private Ewens, stationed at Guichen Bay and who often travelled the Coorong route mentioned a number of wells, including also 'the Chinamans Wells' in 1856. But he certainly gives no indication he thought Chinamans Wells was any different from the others nearby.♦[377] Mention of the name 'Chinamans Wells' of course provides no indication of what kind of well it was at the time.

While a number of wells of various types have acquired the designation "Chinaman's", what is unique about Chinaman's Well on the Coorong is that it is a well-made rounded stone built and capped well, engineered out of the local limestone. An archaeologist's description is:

♦ Ewens accompanied Todd on his survey of the telegraph route the previous year and they probably saw Chinamans Well at the same time.

The well is a round, dome-shaped structure which is capped with a heavy sandstone cover plate through which is cut a small entry hole. The well head stands a mere metre above the ground and was originally encased in a white pipe clay render. Curved blocks were cut in circles carved in layers of limestone on the shore of an adjacent Salt Lake and laid to form a cylindrical casing and shoulder. The thick sandstone cover-plate was also quarried in a similar manner and trimmed to form a tapered profile before being fitted to the well casing.[378]

And in greater detail from the same report:

Well Design
The well, Figure 6, consists of three architectural elements: curved limestone blocks which are assembled to form a perfectly shaped cylindrical casing of four courses below ground level, a dome-shaped shoulder of four courses, and a cover stone. A fixed taper in the shoulder blocks ensures a narrow symmetrical opening at the top of the limestone masonry unit. On the shoulder was placed a round,

wedge shaped cover stone of marine sandstone, weighing an estimated 560 kg, which acts as a keystone to maintain the characteristic "beehive" profile of the masonry above ground. A perfectly round entry hole 43 cm in diameter cut through the cover plate permits draw water to be drawn and periodic maintenance to be carried out. There is no evidence of repair or restoration of the masonry fabric, and, except for two possible old carved initials, the masonry is free of graffiti. The base of the casing rests on a naturally occurring limestone sheet through which a perfectly round hole has been cut to allow ground water to flow up into the well sump. This limestone is identical to the porous masonry blocks used in the well and may itself be a conduit of groundwater through the site. Three sets of opposing toe holes have been cut inside the masonry shell and numerous shallow cut marks on the adjacent surface of the casing indicate either damage from cleaning or attempts to shape the masonry at the time of construction. A white pipe clay renders up to 5 cm thick seals the external casing surface below ground, and, judging from the large amounts of clay scattered around the well, it probably extended over the entire masonry unit up to the cover stone. The render exposed by excavation, Plate 2, is very roughly finished, exhibits no tool marks, appears to be intact, and is still bonded firmly to the casing face. The overall height of the well above the limestone sheet is 1.78 cm and it is 1.65 cm in diameter (OD). Although seasonal changes in ground water may result in fluctuations in water level in the sump, the well's relatively small maximum capacity of about 650 litres suggests that it was designed for human consumption rather than general stock watering purposes.[379]

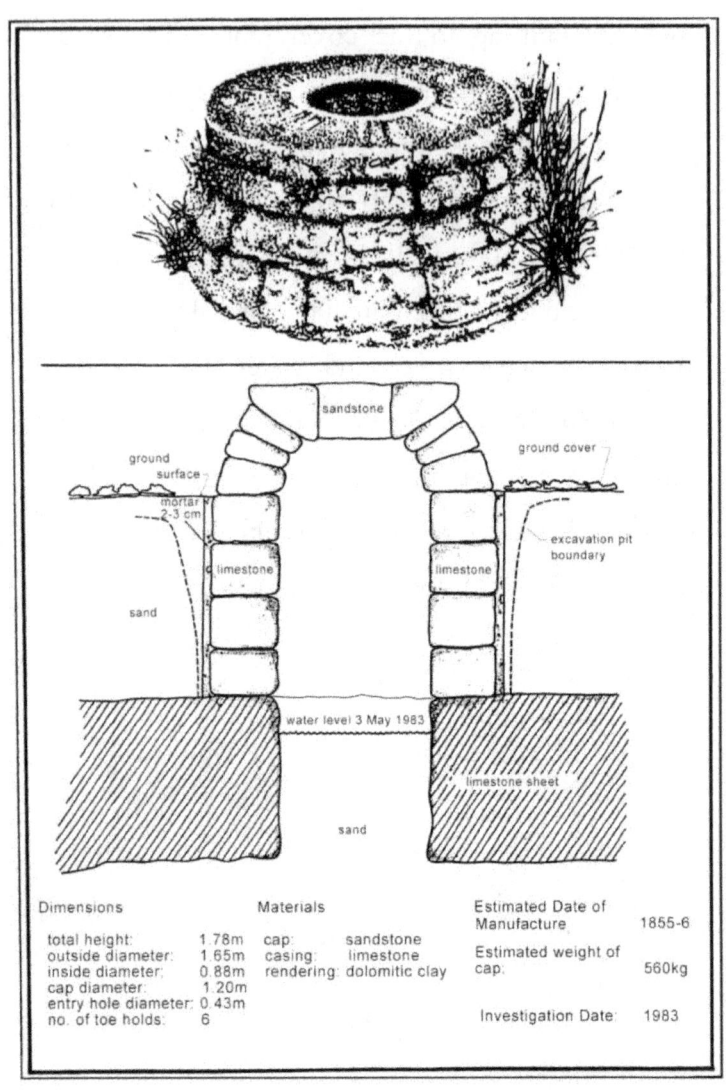

Image 19: Chinaman's Well drawing,
Luebbers, *The archaeology of Chinamans Wells*, p.2.

From this description it is apparent this well is unlike any other well not only in the area, or in South Australia but perhaps anywhere else in the world, including China and Europe. Being of stone or with a stone cap does, however, seem remarkably common on the Coorong and Luebbers found 'three had round or square casings which were made of stone or a combination of stone and concrete blocks, and each had a concrete capping stone'.[380] After inspection Luebbers concluded none of these 'exhibit design characteristics which would necessarily implicate Chinese manufacture' – meaning they were not of the same design as Chinaman's Well, which by making a circular assumption he considered the standard for a Chinese design.[381] One of these wells is pictured in at least two local histories and is assumed to be of the same design, while another round stone well, though without a cap, can be found at Kangaroo Inn.[382] This later looks as old as any these wells to the naked eye but was built within living memory to protect an existing well.♦

All of these wells are consider Chinese built be some and Luebbers also tells of yet another reputed 'Chinese' well that

---

♦ Personal communication to the author from local landowner Roger Andre, April 2022.

191

turned out to be 'a close facsimile of immigrant European wells' as it was rectangular and lined with logs.[383] In fact, wells dug by Chinese market gardeners, who were from the same region of China as the walkers if not the same people, in subsequent years were generally noted as also having 'shallow rectangular wells' and certainly none are recorded as elaborate round stone built in a beehive or stone capped style.[384] Given this uniqueness of design for the Coorong well, attributing its construction to some of the Chinese walkers of 1856 – a well north of Guichen Bay so those arriving directly at Robe in 1857 would not even have passed it – does little to explain its design except to push the mystery further afield.

Luebbers at least makes an effort to explain why a well would be built: 'the arrivals in Adelaide were deliberately setting up a strategy to facilitate the arduous trek overland and this included plans to build a water supply for the expected influx of their Victoria-bound compatriots.'[385] Though why build in a well-watered place with a telegraph line being built along the same route at the time, and why not other wells further back along the route from Adelaide, and why build in such a style all remain a mystery.

The first assumption made by Luebbers and others about this well is that the one mentioned in 1856 as 'at a place called the Chinaman's Wells' was also the stone built well known today. A well reported in 1852 - 'limestone wells' – could be the same and if so was established (in whatever design) before the earliest possible date of Chinese involvement - 1856.[386] Maclaren's report in 1852 of a well that: 'I caused it to be built around with lime-stone' is suggestive, as is the 'sappers built around it with limestone.'[387] This area is called the Limestone Coast and many other wells of more ordinary style used limestone. The ordinary style being round or square but straight down and with no built-up work above ground level and certainly no caps. The use for these wells was usually for animals as well as humans, and water was raised by whip, something impossible with Chinamans Well as it exists today.

When this well is perhaps referred to some twenty years later in 1876, it and several other wells nearby - despite its supposedly unique style - are merely mentioned as 'the wells [that] had been put in thorough repair' by the 'Commissioner of Crown Lands'. There is no hint at anything to distinguish any of these wells from other nearby wells.[388] This could imply that Chinamans Well's in its present form post-dates this repair effort or that another well was being referred to and that under discussion was lost and forgotten in the scrub at that time. Another report in 1876 is obviously referring to a stock well and not the stone construction when it says, 'Chinaman's Well, Wood's Well, and the well at McGrath's Flat all required repairing and fencing round to prevent the sheep trampling them in and consequently filling them up.'[389]

Luebbers also quotes a number of references to Chinamans Wells in this period, including one to the quality of the water but none make mention of anything special about the well itself.[390] Again Luebbers quotes repair at the end of the 19th century of a well at Chinamans Wells that is obviously a whip well for livestock.[391] In fact, the first recorded description of a well that actually identifies or makes any note of its special features is only in 1933:

> One of the strangest is Chinaman's Well, between Salt Creek and Stony Well, and about 40½ miles from Meningie. The top of this well has been carved out of stone with an egg-shaped top so that rabbits cannot topple into it, drown, and foul the water.[392]

There is no mention here of the well actually being built by Chinese people and in fact the first mention of this as an explanation seem to come as late as 1962. This is when a newspaper article describes the well and makes an appeal for information. The problem with such appeals being that someone is bound to jump in. In this case a person described as a 'missionary' born in China declares the well to be of a Chinese style. Given the vacuum in knowledge about the well by that stage many were all too ready to accept this. However, it is interesting to note that the original writer of the article, H. A. Lindsay, does not. Lindsay cannot accept that the walkers would have spent time constructing such a well in 1856 and instead postulates a random Chinese mason building the well at a later date and under government contract.[393]

However, Lindsay was too ready to accept the missionary tale. In reality the woman – Miss R. M. Arnott Rogers – who so positively identified the well style was the daughter of missionaries. Miss Rogers was born in China, in Sichuan and left when she was 9 years of age and was in her 50s when recalling her well technology. Apart from the fact that Sichuan is very far from the Pearl River Delta and has a very different geography it does not in any case have wells remotely like the one on the Coorong, apart from being round and lined with stone. They are neither capped nor built with a beehive structure. The two most unique features of Chinamans Well are therefore not explained.

Having been early named 'Chinaman's Well' it is an easy jump for some to assume it was actually built by Chinese people. Though apparently this was not done until the 20th century. Though why anyone passing through on their way to the goldfields would stop at this one point in a 400 kms walk to build such an elaborate well is a mystery in itself.[♦394] Not to mention the fact that the location is not the most lacking in wells or sources of water. Another basic question is: Is there anything particularly 'Chinese' about this well?

In the ordinary course of things this is where the myth should have remained; a local story believed or not without much evidence either way. The missionary story of the 1960s in fact seems to have been forgotten but the tendency to equate exotic with exotic – the well is different – Chinese people are different – therefore the one built the other – remained. It is at this point that archaeologists in search of an historical

---

♦ As one researcher expressed: 'it seems to be an over investment of time and energy for transient gold seekers'.

explanation arrive on the scene. And once more some 'China experts' are on hand to back up the need for an exotic explanation.

The first to report is William Snoek who in the early 1980s was commissioned to undertake an archaeological survey for the SA National Parks and Wildlife Service. The Service wished to build a 'visitor interpretative centre' for the Coorong National Park focused on Chinamans Well. The well having become an informal tourist site since 1966 and the Lindsay articles apparently.[395] According to this report the area had quite a bit of use starting with a soak that perhaps originally attracted travellers, the well, a 'stock through system', and a 'domestic eating house building complex'. The site was on the Adelaide to Melbourne telegraph line and main route between these cities until 1877, and may have been a 'horse changing station for the stage coach service' as well as an 'eating house'.[396] The passing along this route of Chinese gold seekers is noted and most tellingly that the well is 'in the Chinese style'. The evidence for this is not given apart from a reference to 'Chinese archaeologists.'[397] Even so Snoek only says the well 'may have been' built by the Chinese gold seekers.

Snoek also cites 1864 as a significant year when 'a great deal of public support for the development of navigation through The Coorong' was active and a house was built by 'Joseph Darwent, a prominent Adelaide shipping agent' as a speculative venture.[398] If the supposed 'Chinese style' of the well is put to one side, then this period would seem the most likely for anyone to build an elaborate domestic well at this location. Apparently at least one house was already available for rent in 1864.*[399] A house which is described in an archaeological report as 'made from local limestone, lime-rich mortar, and pipe-clay', and 'finished with dressed stone', that is, with many features similar to the well itself.[400] In addition, in that same year at least one ship was regularly 'navigating the Coorong for 15 miles above Salt Creek to Chinaman's Wells for nine months in the year.'[401] While another observed that: 'In winter boats could go to Chinaman's' Wells, 10 miles above the Salt Creek.' Chinamen's Wells is mentioned in this report as the furthest from Adelaide it would be possible to go via water.[402]

---

* In an aside, the son of the John Gall who advertised a house for rent demonstrated a 'bucket pump' to the visiting Prince George (later George V) in 1881 at Chinamans Well. Though presumably at the stock trough rather than the capped well under discussion.

The 57-footer, "Punkari" famous lake trader sailed to Salt Creek by Charlie Kruse.
—*Godson picture*

Image 20: Coorong boat, *Coorong pilot*, Ronald and Margaret Baker, p.5.

If the well is not in any recognisable Chinese style its nevertheless unique style still requires explanation. A major feature of the well is the millstone-like capstone and how it was excavated from the nearby ground. The reference to Joseph Darwent leads to an advertisement he placed around this time for a 'stone dresser' for the purpose of constructing a 'Country Mill'.[403] While previous to this he had advertised a flour mill with house for rent.[404] Could Darwent have employed this same skilled stoneworker - and the well at Chinamans Well is nothing if not an example of skilled stonework - to construct a well also? This is speculation but is it any less plausible than a Chinese stonemason?

199

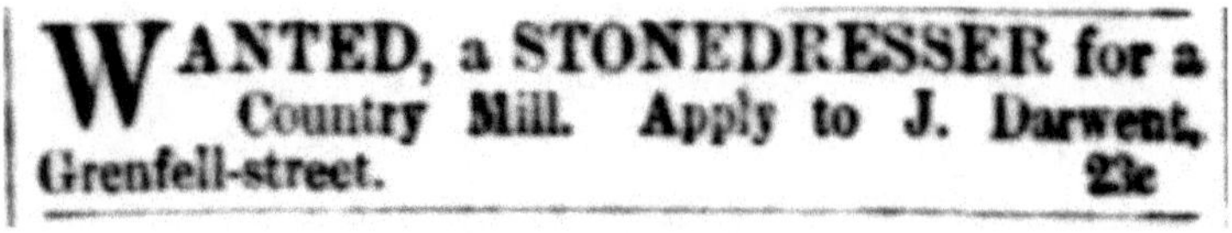

> **WANTED, a STONEDRESSER for a Country Mill.** Apply to J. Darwent, Grenfell-street.
> 23c

Image 21: Stone dresser Ad, *The Express and Telegraph*, 28 January 1867, p.1.

The most thorough report on Chinamans Well is that by Roger Luebbers who having accepted that the well is Chinese then makes strenuous efforts to interpret all the evidence as pointing that way. Thus, when referring to the Raglass 'limestone wells' he dismisses this as evidence that wells existed before 1856 on the basis that there is no reference to Chinese.[405] Luebbers seems to forget that the link to "Chinese" as well builders is to be proven and if the 'limestone wells' are the same wells not yet named 'Chinaman' then this link fails. Luebbers also accepts oral evidence passed from one aged story teller to another of actually seeing Chinese people building the well. The original source would have been a young boy at the time.[406] Without confirmation such a story cannot be given any credence however. This story is further confused by accounts of a Chinese gardener that is said to have had a garden near the well at a later period.[407]

The most startling evidence, still categorised under 'oral history', comes from three 'Chinese officials visiting Adelaide in 1983'. They were supervisors of an exhibition of the Entombed Warriors and inspected the well 'over a picnic lunch'. Described as 'archaeologists directing excavations', presumably in Shaanxi, the three are also described as 'authorities on the design and stylistic characteristics of Chinese architecture in rural China'. Despite Shannxi being a northern province, they apparently felt the well was 'typical of those used in Southern China over the last three centuries.' They were unable to offer a 'detailed explanation of construction techniques' however.[408] It is perhaps right that this evidence remains categorised as "oral history" as no well remotely resembling the well at Chinamans Wells has been found in China and local experts have been as mystified as anyone else around the globe.♦

Despite all these reservations Luebbers comes to an extraordinary conclusion based on his firm assumption that the well is Chinese in style:

♦ Author's personal correspondence with various China-based experts.

The construction of the well at Chinamans Well can be dated with confidence to pre- September 1856 and almost certainly coincides with the landing in South Australia of Chinese gold seekers following legislation in Victoria to restrict Asians from working the lucrative Victorian alluvial goldfields after mid-1855. While neither the exact date of construction nor its social context is recorded, circumstantial evidence suggests that it was the first wave of celestials landing either at Adelaide, or possibly Victor Harbour, which built the wells rather than those that disembarked at Robe when its port facility came on line. Given the scarcity of potable water, Chinese travellers through the Coorong would have difficulty surviving without resorting to local knowledge. It seems most likely then that the Asian visitors were paying Ngarrindjeri land owners for use of their water with metal coins and tokens that were reported by Robert Edwards.[409]

This last reference to payment is a case of speculation piled on speculation – Edwards merely says that the coins found 'may have been payment' for guides or food and water or they 'could have been lost'.[410] Luebbers continues to build his fanciful conclusions, though with a major caveat at the end:

There is prima facia evidence suggesting that more than one well was erected at Chinamans Wells and in addition, the Chinese also built wells at Magrath Flats, Woods Well, and Stony Well. If the force of this testimony is taken as fact, then it must be concluded that the Chinese planned to build an elaborate network of wells to provide a reliable supply of drinking water to a large migration population that was soon to visit the area. The only testimony detailing any specific use of the well by Chinese people indicates that the site was not used at any time for habitation, although it is possible that a Chinese employee at John Gall's Cantara Station may have maintained his personal garden at the well in the late-1890s. The exact relationship of Chinese to the well, its construction details, and the possibly [sic] that substantial Chinese involvement took place was not established by the historic research. Once constructed however, the site as a place name has remained an important landmark until the present day.'[411]

Luebbers does recognise the role of others in the same area and says that: 'Darwent's commercial ventures involving transportation of passengers and cargo via overland and sea routes suggests that the development of Chinamans Wells was a part of a larger plan to cash in on economic growth in the Southeast of South Australia.'[412] Why Luebbers does not consider it was Darwent who might have built the well is another mystery. Though the problem of the unique style the well is constructed in would remain.

Several years after Luebbers report, perhaps around 2001, the South Australian tourism department picked up on the Chinamans Well myth and took it a major step further. They not only began declaring the well was Chinese made but designed a series of elaborate signages which, in the absence of any restraint imposed by evidence, allowed the artist's imagination free reign. This signage includes every cliche and stereotype about Chinese gold seekers that could be imagined.♦[413]

♦ This material is repeated in a pamphlet from Walking South Australia entitled, *Chinaman's Well Historic Site Journey to Gold Walk*, 2020?

Image 22: Fantasy as history, authors photo, April 2022.

All this may well have been a passing fantasy later regretted as the National Parks of South Australia's *Coorong Self-Guided History Trail* pamphlet produced more recently makes no mention of Chinese builders of Chinamans Wells. Instead, this government department's version of history, which nevertheless bravely states that the 'well was built in about 1856', refers only to a 'soak' 'thought to have been established by the Chinese to supply the travelling public with fresh water and vegetables'. This vague statement - for which there is also no evidence - is then followed by a noncommittal (as to actual builders) description of the well itself.[414]

Certainly, researchers such as Penny Paton and H. A. Lindsay did not think this was a Chinese built well.[415] An account quoted by Paton that the well predates the arrival of Chinese gold seekers would appear to be the most plausible. Its name deriving from the subsequent use of the well by a party or parties of Chinese walkers, with perhaps a group that was ill remaining for a longer period so that the name stuck.[416]

The main issues are that the well is not of any known Chinese (or any standard) design, coupled with the fact that the Chinese walkers spending time and energy on its construction is implausible in the extreme. Most fundamentally, the date for the well is wrong with the well reported in 1852 - 'limestone wells' - before the earliest possible date of Chinese involvement - 1856.[417] That the well took on the name 'Chinamans Wells' around the time of the walkers is possible, with some walking from Adelaide that far via the Coorong before turning inland. At this date, however, it is extremely improbable the well was of the same construction as the one touted by SA Tourism today.

All of which leaves the mystery of who did build the well and why in this seemingly unique style. That it was a domestic as opposed to a well for stock is obvious. The location is near a well-used route and a number of residences are reported. The manner of carving out the rounded stone that became the cap is similar to that used to make British millstones. That a mason skilled in millstones but not in wells made Chinamans Well would explain it unique design. That it was constructed when hopes were high for a Coorong water route that did not continue would explain its relative obscurity and the lack of wear on the lip. This is the simplest explanation and thus the safest and most plausible, if not the most interesting or exotic. Just not the stuff the dreams of tourist sign artists are made from unfortunately.

Woolsheds

Chinamans Well on the Coorong is only the most extreme example of what are a surprising number of attributions of workmanship to the walking Chinese gold seekers. Apart from numerous other wells, it seems very common in the western districts of Victoria to hold that various items of infrastructure – woolsheds, dams, stone walls – were also built by the Chinese walkers.♦ Among the most interesting of these are the stone woolsheds built in the 1860s during the boom in wool prices that was one result of the American Civil War and the disruption to cotton exports. The three remaining examples of these imposing woolsheds are all considered by locals to have been Chinese built in some indeterminant manner. Such as always willing to repeat a myth as fact Eric Rolls, 'a woolshed south of Edenhope in Victoria said to have been put up by Chinese coming out of South Australia.'[418] The dates alone make this implausible as the bulk of the 1856-1857 walkers had long passed, leaving only the passengers of the three ships of 1862-1863 as possible woolshed builders at even remotely the correct time.

That the designer and builders of these quite wonderful structures should be relatively unknown is as remarkable as the fact that none appear to have been given any state level heritage recognition or protection as of writing. Nevertheless, there is a contemporary report of the construction of at least one of these still standing woolsheds:

♦ These are largely oral traditions that are still very much alive.
Author's personal interactions in western Victoria, April 2022. Though they also regularly appear in print.

'Mr. Hayman's new woolshed, in course of erection at Lake Wallace' was so noted in mid-1864, a full year after the last shipload of Chinese gold seekers embarked at Robe.[419] As with all the Chinese "walkers as builders" myths no contemporary accounts, including the observers of at least one woolshed's construction, make mention of any Chinese workers even carrying stones let alone as designers or architects. A master stonemason, who was restoring one of the woolsheds, positively identified the design as of standard European style.♦

Image 23: Stone woolshed, western Victoria, authors photo, April 2022

The lack of historical memory as to who did build these woolsheds may hint at a more positive effort at historical

---

♦ Personal communication with Andrew Latta, April 2022.

forgetting. The 1860s was a time when the native people of the western districts of Victoria had not yet been removed to mission stations for their 'protection'.*[420] Those who had survived the massacres and expropriation of their land of the previous generation lived among the white settlers, playing cricket and performing work: 'the blackfellows' services, being required on the station, Edenhope, Lake Wallace, that being shearing time.'[421] It is possible that these same men also worked on building the various woolsheds. Over time the image of indigenous people's existence became problematic and the memory of their labour replaced by a less problematic one - Chinese people. But this is speculative.

Stone Wall – Chinese Wall

Wells and woolsheds are one thing but even more remarkable are the so-called "Chinese Walls" near Dunkeld. These are a remarkable series of dry-stone walls marking boundaries high up the slopes of the Grampians. They are difficult to reach nowadays and like the Chinamans Well their origin seems to have been forgotten. Of course, acquiring a name such as "Chinese Walls" was bound to

---

* The story of Johnny Mullagh & the First XI is well known around Harrow.

create a myth that they are Chinese in origin despite their being of a standard English dry-stone style of construction and like the other infrastructure projects, there being no contemporary mention of Chinese workers – as opposed to walkers – in the area.

As with Chinamans Well on the Coorong the stone walls near Dunkeld have found an academic defender.[422] This time reliance is not on picnicking Chinese curators but rather on the assumption that the mere existence of an oral tradition must be proof of something. This is the "aliens must be out there" argument based on the sheer size of an otherwise empty universe that seems to inevitably result in proof the pyramids were built by spacemen. Thus, having carefully assessed the walls and demonstrated the complete lack of any evidence of Chinese involvement the conclusion that on balance they are of Chinese origin for no better reason than that is what the stories say is disappointing.

Image 24: Stone wall, image courtesy of Timothy Hubbard, Mount Sturgeon's 'Chinese' Wall, p.1.

Unlike the woolsheds and many wells, it seems only this one set of stone walls is attributed to the Chinese walkers. Yet there are many stone walls in Victoria and South Australia of similar style and often with their makers known and no apparent reason why their origin should differ.♦ The Keyneton Station walls built after 1859 for example are attributed to 'the two Tallochs putting up stone walls', according to the journals of Joseph Keynes.[423] Not that this stopped other myths developing such as: 'Myth has it that Australia's stone walls were built by convicts, but it was

---

♦ For example, Point Sturt, Woodchester (aka Tin Pot), Keyneton Station (Pine Hut Rd).

teams of Wallers from Scotland, Wales, Cornwall, Devon and Ireland who plied their skills in the Western District, and taught the locals. Cheaper post and wire fences in the 1880s resulted in a decline in wall building.'[424] Convicts like Chinese walkers are a group to which "old" structures are often attributed by those with no clear idea of when convicts actually did anything. As one account had it, the stone walls of Victoria "were not built by convicts, but by men free and skilled, called Wallers." According to one old such Waller "most of the old Wallers were Irishmen or Scotsmen, very few Englishmen."[425]

The dating of these walls near Dunkeld, like the woolsheds would also seem to be later than the walkers: 'Not until the late 1860s did long stone paddock fences really take off, …'[426] Though there are mentions of some kind of stone walls in the later 1850s, such as references to a house being 'enclosed with a stone wall.'[427] And in 1857 were 'WANTED. TWO MEN competent to build a dry stone wall.' Though this was in Hobart.[428] And in 1862 near Hamilton on the road to Dunkeld along which some of the Chinese walkers probably walked, tenders were 'invited for the ERECTION of Two Miles Dry Stone Wall.'[429] Certainly the opportunity to take up this work was there for the last few shiploads of walkers had they known how to build a dry stone wall, had they been inclined to delay their arrival on the goldfields, and had anyone been inclined to employ them instead of the skilled artisans that were around. Certainly no one commented at the time if they did.

Wells, woolsheds and stone walls (or at least one stone wall) are the major projects often attributed to the Chinese walkers. For completeness' sake a single dam at Muntham and some fretwork on a building are also often mentioned.[430] Though as with the other constructions no contemporary allusions are to be found and the myths seem to have developed only a generation or two later.♦[431]

Explanations

Awareness of the organisation and motivations of the Chinese walkers clearly makes these myths of walls, wells and woolsheds inherently implausible. The various local explanations as to why the Chinese walkers would have spent time building woolsheds or stone walls in whatever capacity reveals just how deep this lack of awareness of

---

♦ Many of these explanations come from local lore rather than written sources. Various conversations while walking Robe to Ararat, April 2022.

planning and incentives is. When pressed to explain why the walkers would have taken up these projects the obvious one of money is also followed by the curious one of constraint. This last shows an awareness of the poll tax itself as part the walkers' motivations, though not of how it worked. A final explanation is that these infrastructure builders were in fact people who did walk to the goldfields but then returned to places made familiar by the walk.

This last explanation appears to be a confusing of the gold seekers generation with a later wave of Chinese market gardeners and other kinds of workers who did begin to populate Victorian rural towns from the 1870s on. Above, the scattered mention of Chinese workers around the colonies of South Australia and Victoria in the 1840s and early 1850s was discussed.✦ Most likely these were indentured workers who came via the Treaty Port of Amoy (Xiamen), though some might also have been from Guangdong via Singapore. After that, Chinese workers (as opposed to gold seekers) do not appear in rural Victoria until the 1860s and these nearly always in the gold districts. It is not until the 1870s and increasingly thereafter that market gardeners and storekeepers of Chinese origin become

---

✦ See pp.16-17.

scattered around the towns and districts through which an earlier generation of people had once walked.

Labour shortage

Certainly, the gold rushes led to labour shortages so that, 'the farmers and squatters of our own western districts, who are always crying out for labour.'[432] A few year before it was observed that: 'Hutkeepers, shepherds, and other labourers are as difficult to be obtained in this Province as in South Australia; all are gold digging mad.'[433] Tolmer also reported coming on 'a 'deserted sheep station' a number of times in his 1852 travels, though whether this was due to labour shortages or other reasons is unclear.[434] Around the Harrow district we saw this led to the employment of local Aboriginal men as shearers.* However, the very same urge to the goldfields that led to these labour shortages was the very same urge that brought Chinese men from their villages, so it is unlikely they would start taking up local jobs just as they were within reach of the goldfields.

Money

Of course, a lack of money forcing just such a delay is plausible and ignorance of the motivations and organisation

---

* See p.210.

of the walkers makes the assumption that the walkers lacked money and therefore would need to work for it a reasonable explanation. However, knowing the credit-ticket system as described above is to understand the implausibility of men anxious to reach the goldfields - men with heavy debts that only successful goldmining could pay off in a reasonable time - stopping to build substantial stone woolsheds or anything else that might take months to accomplish. We also know that the walkers were able to supply themselves with ready cash and even purposely brought knickknacks to sell for this purpose. In all the contemporary accounts of the walkers the only suggestion that any of them did any kind of work for pay were those who attempted to work as 'lumpers' at Port Adelaide, only to be harassed by those used to getting this employment.✦ That similar work, even if only of a short duration, along the routes would not have been commented upon seems unlikely when cooking habits, modes of dress, numbers, guides and other aspects of their walking were all observed and commented on.

Constraint

An even more unlikely explanation as to why the walkers might have worked on major building projects is that they

---

✦ See pp.47-48.

were kept "hostage" by some landowners under threat of being informed on to the Victorian police.[435] This explanation is based on a perception of the Chinese gold seekers as hapless victims liable to tolerate such treatment, ignorance of how the poll tax worked and confusion with later residents' taxes. We have seen above numerous instances of resistance to treatment considered harsh, unfair or illegal, and any "hostage" incidents would have undoubtedly been noted at the time. A basic flaw of the poll tax also discussed above was that crossing via the South Australian land border into Victoria was not illegal and the Victorian police were powerless to do anything.* During the later period 1862-63 arrests were possible and some did take place, though by this stage for non-payment of the resident's tax and never under circumstances that being held hostage for work would have been preferable or tolerated.

All this is not to say that the Chinese walkers would not have been subject to harassment as an account from 1858 demonstrates. In this case it is not the border crossing with South Australia but with NSW and by this time the poll tax has been replaced with a resident's tax. Again, as with the badly drawn up poll tax the police were powerless to enforce

---

* See pp.85-86.

payment if resistance was strong.♥ At the Wodonga crossing they or rather the so called 'Chinese Protector' seems to have resorted to extra-legal harassment in order to obtain the payment. Something the observer takes objection to on grounds of both law and some degree of sympathy for people he considers 'poor' and 'defenceless'.[436]

Describing it as an 'evil practice' in order to extract '£1 per head from all Celestials crossing the overland border into Victoria' we are told they are 'detaining those who are unable or unwilling to pay the tax, until such time as they begin to get hungry'. This informal harassment avoided the need to feed them but ultimately meant they needed to be released after 'four hours in the lock-up'. This was not the only method of harassing Chinese people at the time as they were also liable to pay a tax on any gold they had before leaving Victoria and the same Chinese Protector, a Mr Hanify, was entitled to one-third of any gold confiscated.[437] None of this directly relates to the walkers but if does provide a glimpse into the kind of discrimination and harassment they were walking into.

♥ See pp.88-89.

While the walkers of 1862-63 were relatively few and were also well noted, they found themselves subject to perhaps an even higher level of harassment. However, the arrests that some of them did undergo were rather randomly enacted and by all accounts in the absence of Mr Hanify was not something the Chinese gold seekers feared. They apparently saw their month or so as an enforced period of rest with free food.♦ The only time this came with work was when on one occasion two of the Chinese gold seekers 'being ordered to go with the driver to chop wood in the bush for cooking their meals' even if language barriers made for difficulties and even some amusement. While on another occasion some were sent to Portland where they helped in the development of the local botanical gardens.♣[438] That these later walkers could or did develop such a fear of incarceration that they would allow themselves to be forced to work on stone walls or woolsheds and that this was never commented upon at the time is unlikely in the extreme.

What is more likely is that a later generation, either misremembering or misinterpreting, confounded the various forms of harassment. This is particularly likely as the

---

♦ See above p.89.
♣ See p.43.

memory faded of a police force and government willing to do this extra-legal harassment. Instead, such behaviour is more easily attributed to random unnamed settlers.

Returnees and new arrivals

A final explanation that attempts to better fit with some of the dates of infrastructure construction that are took place after the walkers had past is that any Chinese involved were ex-walkers. That is, they were returnees from the goldfields who for whatever reason – good experiences, familiarity, contacts – had decided to take up work in areas they had walked through years before. Another alternative is: "A few stopped, found work and made their homes in isolated areas and towns along the way."♦[439] This brings us to the question of whether any Chinese people ever worked in the Western Districts of Victoria. The answer being that of course they did, but also that nearly all are from the 1870s at the earliest and always as individuals or in small numbers scattered as market gardeners mostly.

The appearance of people of Chinese heritage in Victoria as workers other than gold miners begins gradually in the 1860s and while it is perfectly possible that some were in fact ex-

---

♦ What evidence there is for this is unknown.

gold miners who may have arrived originally as walkers via South Australia there is no evidence concerning this. More significantly, even if they were, there is nothing to link these Chinese people to the various infrastructure projects such as woolsheds or stone walls. In fact, the only link would appear to be that they are Chinese and in the various 'oral' accounts that circulate Chinese Australians of the last 30 years of the 19th century are readily conflated with the walkers of the mid-19th century. The final aspect to note is that considering Chinese people at any time in the 19th century as 'Chinese Australians' was not common and this 'othering' made/makes the conflating easier.

1860s

Lack of context in the history has 'forgotten' the pre-gold rush Amoy labourers: 'They had at one time a number of Asiatic, and they were told that they answered well as shepherds'; and the post-goldrush presence from the 1860s on.*[440] As far as Chinese workers doing anything outside of goldmining is concerned the earliest account is 1863, in the goldfields areas, where we have: 'Mongolian Sheepshearers. —According to the Ararat Advertiser, some of the local squatters have commenced employing Chinamen as

---

* For Amoy people see above p.17.

shearers, and it appears from the reports which reach us that the experiment has proved eminently successful.'[441] While, a Dunkeld based writer did speculate in 1864 that 'Chinese labour could be had reasonable enough'. It is not clear why he thought this, perhaps thinking of the shearers, but his belief they were skilled in cotton growing or silk does not indicate he saw them doing anything else and certainly not building dry stone walls, etc.[442] A little later, in 1867, there is a report of the harvest being successful – 'thanks to the Chinese element' – with this still well within (Ascot) the goldfield districts themselves.[443] The first mention of Chinese people outside the goldfields districts appears in 1868 when it is reported that the 'commercial John Chinaman has found his way to Portland' 'hawking goods through the town' and being 'an object of interest and wonder' to 'small boys' at least.[444]

1870s

While it is likely these shearers and hawkers were ex-miners or even still miners supplementing their income in the dry season, most of the Chinese workers from the 1870s on were just as likely to be part of a second wave of Chinese arrivals that has been largely forgotten. In fact, it was the increase in Chinese arrivals after the post-gold rush decline that led to agitation and a renewal of poll taxes in 1881. Analysis of CEDT (Certificate Exempting the Dictation Test) files shows that people of Chinese birth living and working in western Victoria at the beginning of the 20th century were nearly all middle aged or younger.* That is, they were born around 1860 to 1870 at the earliest and likely to have arrived in Australia as young men in the 1880s or thereafter.[445]

As far as localities in the western districts of Victoria along the routes of the gold seeker walkers are concerned, the earliest report is from 1874 when a man named Ah Yuk won 'seven prizes of £1 each for vegetables and fruit' at the Hamilton Agricultural Show.[446] Later that same year some prospective market gardeners arrived in Coleraine 'looking out a suitable piece of land to put to the use of vegetable growing'.[447] This they apparently did and by the following year they were celebrating a 'New Year's Day feast' to which they 'invited many of their customers to attend and partake of the good things provided'.[448] This perhaps became a regular occurrence or at least was repeated the following year, when Ah Fie and his company hosted another New

---

* CEDT's were issued by the Commonwealth government to pre-1901 residents so they could re-enter Australia if they wished. Being otherwise unable to if not white enough and so subject to the fake Dictation Test.

Year dinner.[449] At this time the market gardeners at both Hamilton and Coleraine, which included Germans as well as Chinese, are reported to have been quite competitive.[450]

Just across the border in Penola, SA Chinese vegetable growers had also recently set themselves up so that by 1878 it was reported to be 'scarcely worthwhile growing vegetables, as our local Chinese raise everything we want at a very reasonable rate, and bring it round to the door.'[451]

1880s

The market gardeners at Coleraine and Hamilton in the 1870s would appear to have been working for themselves. In 1880 Moy Hing, although working as a gardener also, was employed by a W. Moodie at Wando Dale, though Moy Hing apparently threw in rain prediction for free.[452] In this period lone men of Chinese origin were perhaps not uncommon and the death of one such person near Dunkeld who could not be identified was reported without much excitement.[453] While Hamilton and Coleraine seems to have been well supplied with vegetables for many years by the mid-1880s, Harrow somewhat further west of the goldfields, considered itself fortunate it seems when a Chinese market gardener 'settled on the banks of our river' and 'commenced gardening operations'. It seems for those without their own garden's vegetables were 'very scarce'. Nevertheless, this acknowledged dependence on the skills of Chinese people to 'procure vegetables at a reasonable price' did not inspire the writer to enquire the name of the individual gardener nor stop his being referred to as simply a "Heathen Chinee".[454] Similarly when praising the irrigation efforts of the market garden at Coleraine in 1887, the writer referred to these possessors of 'considerable forethought' as 'Celestials gardeners' - it was considered sufficient.♦[455]

If Harrow was only just receiving some Chinese residents, Horsham not only had had many for a while but was by the mid-1880s turning them into citizens, or at least British subjects:

> Four Chinese at Horsham, named Lee Gee Kwong, a herbalist♣, Choong Ah Chee, Lee Tew Hack, and Sue Ah Toy, were on Friday brought by Mr Lee Young, Chinese interpreter, of Deep Lead, before Mr, Hutchinson P.M,

---

♦ For more on labelling rather than naming see, Michael Williams, 'Vegetables varied and excellent, chiefly from a Celestial Garden', *History*, September 2022, pp.9-11.
♣ Lee Gee Kwong had been a doctor in the district since 1876.

to take the oath of allegiance for letters of naturalisation.[456]

These four who applied to be naturalised were in addition to at least four more - Ching Wot, Ah Pay, Wah Chan and Ah Me - who were working on a market garden on the Wimmera River at Horsham around this period.[457] Horsham was not necessarily on the Robe to goldfields route and Warracknabeal, where Chung Yet and Chang Lee lived at this time, was far off any such route.[458] Whether ex-miners or new arrivals in the colony, these Chinese men were seeking out opportunities all over rural Victoria rather than fondly remembering any experiences they may or may not have had on their walk in 1856 or 1857.

Market gardens run by groups of Chinese men – such as that of 'Ah Wan, Ah Chin, Sun Kwong War, Ah Chum, Ah Chung' near Hamilton or that described as 'a regular oasis in a desert' near Casterton seemed to have been plentiful by the mid-1880s.[459] We have the names of the men gardening near Hamilton because they were applying for gardening licences (a peculiarity of the Colony of Victoria unknown elsewhere) whereas those winning prizes at Coleraine are listed next to their named European-heritage competitors as simply 'some of the Chinese gardeners' or 'a number of Chinese gardeners'.[460] Similarly at the Harrow Flower Show in 1887, while the prize for best turnips was won by Mrs Broughton, cabbages or shelled peas was won by a Fulham or Harrow 'Chinese gardener'.[461]

Not all were gardeners, and Hong Sip worked at Muntham station as a cook as well as having a wife named Margaret who lived in nearby Cavendish. Hong Sip was the unfortunate victim of a beating from which he subsequently died.[462] Such a death of course raises the question of prejudice and hostility but it should always be remembered that such tragic cases as Hong Sip's is the stuff of newspapers.

A reminder that the 'Chinese Question' was a contested one comes from a debate on the Chinese Poll Tax at Harrow a few years after the unfortunate Hong Sip's death. The debate is meant as an amusement and the nearly even vote on the question of repeal is perhaps more an indication as to the entertainment of the speakers than its serious consideration. Nevertheless, the various points made do tell us something of what ideas of Chinese people were floating around at this time. Thus, we have that, 'they made excellent husbands;

that they never sue for divorces, and are very kind' (Hong Sip had perhaps been separated from Margaret but not divorced). That Chinese people had 'honesty and industrious habits', and China produced tea (though a counter argument asserted ladies tea drinking at one 'another's place' was 'the root of many disturbances'). That 'the Chinese had a great weakness for the European's poultry' while 'China was a great and civilized empire many years before Britain'. From personal experience they were 'as honest (if not more so) than Europeans' and those that 'employed Chinese labourers' felt that the 'fellows gave satisfaction.'[463] This mix of positives and negatives is of course characteristic of opinions based largely on stereotypes and generalisations.

It is this tendency to generalise about 'Chinese', even to the extent of failing to name prize winners, or to continually give such descriptions as: 'premises occupied by four Chinamen'♦ that perhaps helps explain the origin of the many myths and their persistence.[464] In the absence of much detailed awareness the lives of Chinese people of the late 19th century in the districts of Western Victoria, their conflation with the more well-known, if still garbled, history of the Chinese walkers of the goldrush era is easily understood.

♦ Referring to hawkers of vegetables living in Narracoorte.

While the CEDT records and newspaper reports cited above indicate most Chinese people in the western districts came well after the period of the gold walkers from Robe. This is not to say that some from this period did not remain. The 70-year-old gardener who was flooded out at Harrow in 1906 was certainly old enough to have been just such an ex-walker.[465] As was perhaps the 78-year-old station cook – known imaginatively as "Dummy" due to his being deaf and dumb – who died that same year after 40 years in the district.[466] But such scattered possibilities do not amount to masonry woolshed builders or stone wall layers.

That gangs of Chinese workers did operate and accomplish much in for example NSW and Queensland as scrub cutters is well known, as are their efforts in the Northern Territory in various occupations.[467] That similar occurred in western Victoria at an earlier date without being commented by upon at the time is fanciful. Of course, individuals could do anything but all that can be said is no evidence exists that would mitigate the inherent implausibility.

Return

A final reason why these various myths are so implausible is readily understood when the final leg of the journey for most is considered. This was of course the return to family in the village. While not all did so, most certainly did – it was after all their intention on setting out. The return journey was not of course via Robe but simply down to Port Philip and hence to Hong Kong and to the village. Those that took up occupations as vegetable hawkers or market gardeners could have been older men direct from the gold fields, or men who were setting out again from the villages after a period home, or a second generation inspired by the examples of their fathers and uncles, or even those who came for the short-lived Queensland Palmer River goldrush of the 1870s who then headed south in search of income.♦

♦ For a detailed account of what was a three-generation lifestyle see, Michael Williams, *Returning Home with Glory*, University of Hong Kong Press, 2019.

(11) So, there you are - Why myths and why they persist?

Having examined these myths and stereotypes it is relevant to ask why they exist in the form they do and why have they persisted? The answers to both questions are enlightening in that they speak to a range of perspectives that centre on white Australia and its historical whitewashing that combine to create and maintain a victimhood narrative that simply cannot be justified by the history.

It is indicative that none of the stories or accounts of Chinese people building anything arise until the late 19th or early 20th century. That is, at least one and usually two generations after the events they refer to. Some of these accounts come from stories told by people claiming to be eye witnesses, but are more often their children's re-telling's, as well as various newspaper accounts – usually without acknowledged sources – recapping the most dramatic aspects of the history many years after the events. Local historians often repeat these accounts with little questioning as to their origin or plausibility. Most dangerously many even sceptical researchers assume these oral tradition and myths "must" have a core of truth even if they are exaggerations or otherwise incorrect. A flair for the dramatic and a persistent "Chinese as victims" perspective providing much reinforcement.

It is also indicative that when these later accounts are based on actual aging eye witnesses, they do not mention the features common in the myths. Thus, one account from 1910 reportedly based on the writings of an eyewitness was that 'Dunkeld [Mt Sturgeon] was used as a camping place by those travelling overland from Adelaide to the diggings. The Chinese came over in great numbers, one company consisting of 1100 Celestials, and the local store did a thriving trade in rice and sugar.'[468] No mention of the 'Chinese Wall' or its supposed erection by Chinese walkers or otherwise by someone who was actually there at the time. Instead, we have a name (just when these stone walls came to be called 'Chinese Walls' is unknown) and a lack of knowledge of who built them or even exactly when. This is a vacuum in our knowledge that some cannot resist filling regardless of plausibility.

Perhaps the real mystery is why so many infrastructure projects of the mid-19th century have apparently been forgotten enough that their builders are no longer known?

Mythologising – the process

The origin of most myths can be seen to be, as previously argued, ignorance and lack of context combined with a favouring of the dramatic. Of these the foremost is a confusion over the difference between oral history and oral accounts or folklore. Oral history is the use of interviews and evidence acquired orally in an effort to build up a picture of the history. Ideally it is concerned with people's memories of things they actually experienced. Even if this were imposed as a rigid definition the evidence of memories and personal bias would still be problematic and need careful sifting. However, as such shifting is also required of documentary evidence this is simply part of the historiographical process.

Quite another level of credibility comes into play however when discussing oral accounts or what can be considered folklore. This is to say, stories and explanations of things passed around from person to person of unknown origin. Two assumptions are often made about such accounts. The first is that they "must" contain a kernel of truth and the second that they gain in credibility once written down. Both these assumptions are patently false. Such stories can of course be entirely baseless and unless corroborating evidence is found need to be treated as such. The fact that a story concerning events 100 years ago was written down say 50 years ago does not make it documentary evidence. Yet this is exactly how many of these accounts are treated.

An interesting example of this process is a document entitled, "Transcribing and Editing of audio tape of Monthly meeting held on 5th November, 1990 – The Chinese Invasion." This was a meeting of members of the Dunkeld and District Historical Museum that was recorded and subsequently transcribed. In this meeting those present either summarised some of the published accounts mentioned above as unreliable, or recounted their own stories passed to them either from local or family lore.♦ As such it is an interesting record of the myths concerning the Chinese walkers current in 1990 but cannot be considered a source of any history as such. Yet very often such material is accepted as a "source" with the assumption that something must lie at their root.♣ Thus, the meeting at Dunkeld recorded stories of the uniqueness of Chinese mining shafts,

---

♦ Such as Cawthorne, Ellen Mary, *The Long Journey* and Sprengel, *Robe's Chinese invasion.*
♣ This is a possible source for Ritchie, *Guichen Bay to Canton Lead.*

235

some remembrance of various Chinese vegetable hawkers, an account of a Chinese person killed for his pigs, reference to the Mt Sturgeon 'stone fence' – notably not then referred to as the Chinese Wall – which is attributed to 'either Chinese or Scots', and finally a bizarre story of 14 Chinese walkers somehow forced to build 'stone houses' in which they were then imprisoned.[469]

At this same meeting in Dunkeld was Ian MacKinnon who claimed his grandfather Angus MacKinnon was a 'mailman between Penola and Guichen Bay' from 1854 to 1861. Presumably based on recollections of his grandfather's account he outlined a summer 'shortest line' from Penola through Bogalara, Tallangower, Gray's Crossing (of the Gleneng River), Chetwynd, Koolomert, Wando Vale [Dale?] and Coleraine. Winter rains necessitating 'longer routes'. The route Ian MacKinnon claims to have from his grandfather is in fact more circuitous than the direct one from Penola to Coleraine so he may in fact have confused this with the wet winter route.[470]

This MacKinnon account also claims Chinese walkers built Muntham Dam and an embankment at Chetwynd Station. While others 'never, ever, got to the goldfields', instead becoming station cooks.⁴⁷¹ All the stations and other locations mentioned in the account are recorded in the newspapers of the 1850s and 1860s, however never in relation to Chinese workers, whether as dam builders or cooks. It was not until a generation later from the 1870s afterwards that such places acquired Chinese cooks and other types of workers. For people such as Ian MacKinnon recollecting the words of grandfathers many years after their death this collapsing of time is all too easy. Such confusing of stories and times is understandable, less understandable is the ready acceptance of these as historically accurate regardless of their inherent implausibility.

Of course, grandfathers don't necessarily get it wrong every time – or rather their grandsons in the retelling – and the retelling by Mr C. E. Block of his grandfather George Sowden's account of interacting with the Chinese walkers at Harrow is perhaps a case in point. According to his grandson George Sowden '1000 Chinese had arrived in Harrow' and 'pitched tents on the wooded slopes of the town'.

> Mr Block said his grandfather had met a Chinese who owned a neat pair of scales to be used for weighing gold and had asked him if he could buy them. "What do you

want for it?" - "Ten shillings." The Chinese had made a neat parcel for him which he had proudly taken home. But at home he found the package to be empty and when he returned to the camp all the Chinese inevitably looked the same.[472]

This account is more plausible because it specifies a personal experience that is both probable and not stereotypical. In fact, its balancing of the usual "Chinese as victim" narrative so popular with the myths with a Chinese as sharper makes it more plausible. Of course, to assume from this that all the walkers were willing and able to defraud people would be as false a conclusion as that of assuming all their guides were false or that all starved along the way.

Coleraine Historical Society has also carefully preserved the stories and myths that circulate locally but by writing them down without comment or context have not so carefully preserved the history. On file with this society is a document entitled "Chinese at Coleraine" in which is listed a mix of quotes from books, oral accounts and names of Chinese people. Thus, we have 'Tim Laidlaw said' the well-known Kim family built 'the homestead and woolshed' at Runnymede Station in the 1860s.[473] Well known the Kim family may have been but that the first Kim, Meng Kim was born in 1865 makes his capacity to build anything at that time unlikely. This is one myth that could not take flight due to the history and arrival of Meng Kim in the area being relatively well known and accessible.

Less easy to dismiss is: 'Albion [a local newspaper?] 10th January 1957 refers to the construction of dam on Muntham station by Chinese labourers, now known as Chinamen's Dam on J R Shady's property Avalon.'[474] This is the oldest reference to this now persistent myth with its very vagueness – What dam? When was it built? – helping it survive despite its inherent implausibility. Implausible because the dam was well known, with Bonwick describing the property in 1857 as: 'The pride of the whole is *Muntham*, the most beautiful station in Victoria.'[475] As was the presence of the walkers, 'one hundred and seventy-five Chinese called a few days ago at Muntham,'[476] Yet no one linked the two at the time.

A stone dam at Muntham was swept away in 1861.[477] If the construction of the Muntham Dam referred to was its replacement then this was done after the bulk of the walkers had passed. Leaving the three shiploads of 1862-63 to do all the work once again. There is even evidence that the dam or a dam at Muntham was paid for by ratepayers via the Dundas

Roads Board. The likelihood that such a body paid Chinese workers without comment at the time being extremely low.[478] A dam at Muntham is again mentioned a few years later in connection with a reservoir 'constructed under the superintendence of Mr C. M'A. King. The water is supplied from a large reservoir confined by a dam.'[479] Again no hint of the involvement of exotic labour of any kind then, nor when the Muntham estate was being subdivided in 1901, when its 'very large dam' and the estate's 50-year history was being referred to.[480]

The failure to mention Chinese workers is not direct evidence of course. But the appearance of the suggestion of their building a dam only several generations afterward the event when contemporary accounts do not, make for myth not history. Myths fit the stereotypes: How many of those who confidently relate the dam building Chinese story remember for example the regular visits to Coleraine of the Hamilton-based herbalist Hew Chee as recently as 1918?[481]

Dubiousness of oral accounts
Accounts based on memories of past times even those passed down within families are problematic and inclined to be given far more credence than they deserve. An example of

problems even after a single generation are the accounts of Thomas Smeaton, who was a near contemporary of the walkers. Though he is often mistakenly thought to have been in Robe at the time of the walkers. Smeaton did live in Robe in the period soon after the walkers and so was presumably in a position to have heard the accounts of eyewitnesses.♦

Yet Smeaton, despite his proximity in time, like many afterwards, seems unaware of the many hundreds of Chinese gold seekers who arrived in Robe in 1856 via coastal steamers and so considers the arrival of the *Land o' Cakes* in early 1857 with its over '500' – actually less than 300 – Chinese passengers as a surprise 'invasion'.[482] This characterisation – so often taken up in newspaper headlines – contrasts strongly with a contemporary report that describes the arrival of this ship and a number of others in which the disembarkation of so many Chinese passengers are described as creating only a 'more than usual degree of activity'. Activity which is also associated with 'the greatly increased traffic in wool'.[483]

♦ Many mistake Smeaton for an eyewitness, e.g., Horsfall, *March to Big Gold Mountain*, p.25.

It is this same Smeaton who also claims '1 women', and that 'many died', and repeats the stories of overcharging for landing and rough handling. He may also be the origin of the story of the 'more than one case (it is said) the "Pilot" led them a day or two's journey into the wilderness, and then – bolted!' He also makes a rare mention of accommodation in detail: 'The tents were stretched over a horizontal pole supported by two pairs of crossed bamboos. A tent of about 10ft x 6ft sufficed for six men.'[484] This is a mixed bag of the plausible and the implausible and as Smeaton is a re-teller of stories of proven unreliability in at least one instance nothing he says should be taken as evidence unless corroborated.✦

An actual eyewitness, albeit retelling from memories some 60 years old or more, is Charles Savage. His dates may be wrong but his account can be more readily accepted if for no other reason than that Charles sticks to the plausible. Thus, while describing the walkers as 'undisciplined hordes' that 'made living precarious' he recalled 'a big camp' into which he and a friend 'slipped across one night and cut the ropes of several of the tents. The Chinamen swarmed out like ants and gave chase, each man carrying a knife'. Charles also

---

✦ Sprengel, *Robe's Chinese invasion*, p.19, repeats all this without hesitation however.

mentioned that the 'Chinamen gathered a green weed which grew on the rocks near the beach and ate it like cabbage'. Most noteworthy is his mention of hiring people to carry baggage, not guides and certainly no mention of Smeaton's abandonments. Instead: 'The method they adopted to reach the goldfields in Victoria was by hiring horse and bullock teams to carry their baggage across the border, the men travelling on foot. In those days many bullock teams carted wool from the South-East country and Victoria to Robe.'[485]

Joseph Verco is another often cited as an eye witness to the Chinese arrivals in Adelaide, yet as he was born in 1851, he could have only been 5 or 6 when they were most active. In fact, his account of exchanging Chinese coins for pennies and 'drowned Chinamen' appear to be mostly a retelling of the stories of others. Verco was a well-known medical personage and his records in the South Australian library are in an easily readable script. Both factors seem to account for his being cited over any inherent value in his observations or the more plausible but less well-known Charles Savage.[486]

Not only is Thomas Smeaton not an eyewitness but he is also an early (first) example of efforts to make the history 'dramatic' while neglecting anything as mundane as successful walking or being well organised. Chroniclers of later generations had even more difficulty balancing the mundane with the dramatic and local Robe historian Roland Campbell, who had a more serious relationship with historical investigation, belatedly recognised the possibility of what today would be called 'false memory'. The description of his efforts at eliciting eye witness reports is highly instructive of the unreliability of oral accounts.

> I showed what I had written to another from Robe who was younger than myself. In the story a pitched battle was referred to with their bamboo poles. The reader of my notes said he remembered seeing the fracas, and could hear the clashing of the bamboo poles in his mind still. The only Chinamen to which the story could apply only came in in such numbers (15 to 1600) which composed the belligerents came in in about the middle of 1857. My reader was born in July 1862! Another to whom I was speaking about the arrival of the celestials told me that he remembered them passing through Penola in hundreds one after the other like a lot of ducks, with their bamboo poles and baskets on their shoulders, I quietly interrogated, "When were you born?" and he replied "In 1874." quite composedly, I responded, "The Last Chinamen came in through Robe in 1863," He replied with astonishment, "Why! that was eleven years before I was born." So, there you are.[487]

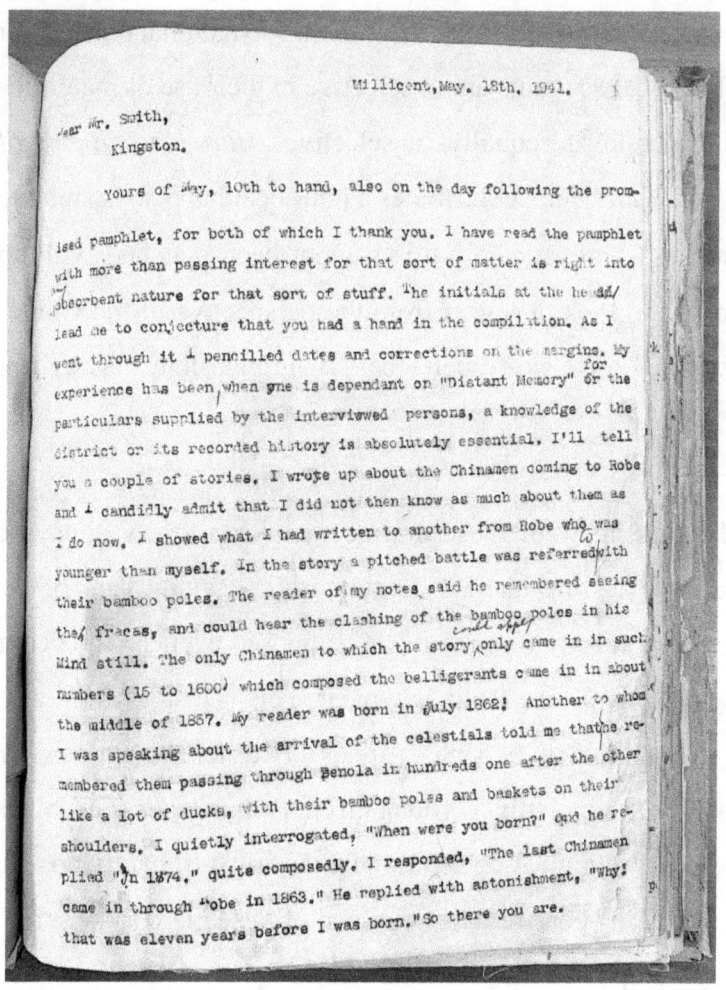

Image 25: Notes on oral accounts, Letter to Mr Smith, Kingston, 18 May 1941, Millicent, State Library of South Australia, PRG 497.

In the second half of the 20th century the local historians of Robe have continued to perpetuate the dramatic story of thousands of "exotic" arrivals at their tiny port featuring it as a major event – nearly always an 'invasion' – in the local history and one of Robe's few claims to national recognition. The local accounts are unselective in their use of material as is Horsfall's equally unselective *March to Big Gold Mountain* which contributes a non-local but also dramatized effort.♦ Unfortunately this has not been matched with any effort to look at things from the perspective of the Chinese walkers and so much that is implausible passes into "history".

In fact, many of these oral accounts can nearly always be traced back to a late 19th century origin, leaving a gap of over 30 years from the time of the supposed events. An account accepted by Eric Rolls is typical. This is a story from a 90-year-old told in the 1980s supposedly from the man's mother who was reputedly a 'young girl in Penola when the Chinese came through'. A connection that is only just barely possible even if the possibility of the kind of false memory described by Campbell is not considered.[488]

Of course, local historians and story tellers such as Eric Rolls are not the only ones to take oral accounts too seriously. Roger Luebbers was a professional archaeologist but in

---

♦ Despite its title only the first two of its 13 chapters refers to the Robe Walk.

using oral history he makes the same mistake. In interviewing people about the wells of the Coorong he readily dismisses the fact they think all the wells are of Chinese origin but accepts it when they say the well at Chinamans Wells is. Here he is merely accepting what accords with his preconceptions. The fact that all agree with the undisputed fact that the well 'is unique in design' is presented as reenforcing this in some way.[489] Another well-related piece of local folklore that declared it Chinese in origin turned out to be typical of 'immigrant European wells'.[490] Yet other oral accounts are accepted by Luebbers when they suit.

Timothy Hubbard, a heritage consultant makes a similar mistake by seeking to explain an oral account rather than prove it.[491] His there "must" be something behind folklore approach – which Campbell disproves – inevitably makes everything and anything possible. Thus, Hubbard in declaring the stone walls near Dunkeld to be probably Chinese built fails to consider the many other stone walls of Victoria, and fails to considered the inherent implausibility of the Chinese gold seekers stopping for any length of time to do any such work. He also fails to consider that the walkers were in debt, that gold was their aim, and that

Dunkeld was very close to their destination and thus one of the least likely places to waste time learning to build stone walls of a kind totally absence in their place of origin, the Pearl River Delta. Hubbard also fails to consider that the walkers from Adelaide and Robe of 1856 and 1857 and the relative handful of 1862 and 1863 were well documented and intensely observed. Many comments of their passing were made, while not a single contemporary report refers to any of them building stone walls, woodsheds or stone wells.

Such stories really only begin to enter the record in the 1890s when only the vaguest details of the Robe walkers were still remembered, or who built stone walls either it seems. Hubbard is aware that Chinese gardeners and other types of workers do enter the rural districts of Victoria in the 1870s but sees this as a continuity rather than a new wave and so conflates them with the unrelated gold seekers of a previous generation. He specifically mentions Chinese sheep washers of the 1870s and assumes them to be a direct link with the walkers of 15 or more years previously. Finally, Hubbard, like many, seems to believe that oral myths get stronger and more real as a result of mere repetition or worse, printing.

Finally, many oral accounts, such as those picked up by Ritchie in her 2004 publication are then quoted without analysis in other documents such as an Ararat heritage study or pasted into a website. Thus the, at best, remembering's of a story by an old man told to them in their youth by another old man remembering his youth becomes quotable "history".

Context

Once these myths or at least certain perspectives are established they in turn determine the selection of sources that best re-enforce these. To give an example, it is often related that the gold diggings were made up of a diverse range of people and Chandler's memoir is often quoted to illustrate this, speaking of Bendigo he says:

> There were lawyers, doctors, tradesmen, and labourers, of every nation and of every shade. There was the black Negro and the fair Norwegian alongside one another; there was the noble of England and the escaped slave of America …[492]

Yet Chandler also goes onto to give a much less quoted account of conflict among these groups that provides a valuable counterpoise to the oft told Chinese-related conflicts. This is an account of a 'lot of Tipperary men' who attempted to keep a digging to themselves. Another group of miners armed themselves and 'drove off all the Tips', including that 'one or two died'. Later a group of 40 Chinese diggers were also prevented from joining this digging.[493] This is not to deny the widespread anti-Chinese violence but merely to give it its violent context:

> Case of 'professional jumpers' in Clunes that 'were rushed by a crowd of miners who' had 'some pitch ready prepared'. The pitch was 'hot and handy' and the jumper, a 'Mr Black, was stripped and made as black as his name'. 'Feathers not being handy the miners stuck him over with straw, leaves and twigs, and after a time let him go.' Mr Black, 'had himself photographed and 'has commenced legal proceedings against the Company, damages £1,000.'[494]

Without context a great deal relating the Chinese walkers is easily misinterpreted especially in regard to the selection of sources. This was seen with the account of illness among the walkers given by the Chinese Protector and of those thrown overboard when landing at Guichen Bay.[♦] In both instances

---

[♦] See pp.172-173 and pp.167-167.

a rare event was transformed by lack of context into a typical happening.

Culture

A powerful aid to mythmaking is course ignorance, particularly of the culture and motivations of those being mythologised. Thus, even the lump sum term "Chinese" is misleading in a people for whom local dialect/language and family like relations were so important. It was seen earlier in the account given by Edward Hearne how these relations so greatly influenced the assistance an individual might receive regardless of the perception that they were all "Chinese".◆ For most of the observers we are forced to reply on these distinctions are missed or misunderstood. The following is a rare instance of the observation of difference, yet it is still very much an outsider view that limits the value of what we are being told:

> The men who are now arriving are from the neighbourhood of Canton, and are of a different race from those who came last season; their complexions are much darker, and they appear, as a general rule, to be much more powerfully built. Their equipment

◆ See pp.138-139.

is very complete, and they are well provided with money. Their proceedings are characterised by great, exactitude, and their encampments are neat and orderly."[495]

Victimisation

A great deal of the acceptance of these myths lies in the perception of the Chinese gold seekers as hapless victims from an inferior race. This is a perception that evolved towards the end of the 19th century as part of the justification for the growing White Australia policy and it can be seen to linger in these accounts. These are accounts that highlight deaths but not success, assaults but not resistance, that perpetuate stereotypes of dog eating and stolid endurance but not of operatic entertainments or festivities. To this can be added a sense of exoticism which also has 'the Chinese' building woolsheds or anything else the origin of which is now forgotten or not immediately apparent.

♣ It is tempting to say these are descendants of the Manchu Bannerman settled at Canton, and therefore what Dundas Crawford identified on the Victorian goldfields as 'Tartars'. But this is speculation and they may merely have been a better fed group from the city rather than the villages. See Michael Williams, 'Observations of a China Consul', *Locality*, Vol. 11, no.2, 2000, p.5.

White Australia Policy - I

One of the most telling aspects is the point in time of the origin of most of these myths. The lack of any hint of them at the time the events occurred is of course decisive. This is particularly so when it is considered that accounts of the Chinese gold seekers were widespread and their doings reported in detail. It is only a generation or some 30 years or more after that retellings of the trek to the goldfields begin to appear, many peppered with a variety of dramatic features for the first time. It is significant that these retellings of the 1880s and after are at a time of renewed discussion over Chinese immigration and the proposed and then actual new discriminatory laws. The Guichen Bay trek in this context serves as a warning of Chinese perseverance and capacity to evade laws that are only enacted in a single colony. For these purposes, knowledge of the organisation of this trek is not relevant or even runs counter to a focus on the "inferiority" of the people being discussed. The successful nature of the endeavour is better put down to a stolid strength which in the context of fear of low wages or business competition is also deemed a negative attribute or a danger to be guarded against. Thus, the evolving White Australia policy helped to create myths of victimhood and weakness and at the same time of hard work and perseverance that was also a negative.

The myth of the Lambing Flat riots are perhaps the most well-known result but the Robe Walk is of a similar origin and nature.[496]

In 1897 the link between late 19th century White Australia Policy fears and the Robe walkers was made plain: 'I wonder how many people who talk of a possible Chinese invasion of Australia know that there was such an invasion more than forty years ago.'[497] What follows is an account which includes stories of overcharging and false guides, as well as exaggerated numbers – 25,000 – while being ignorant of how or why, apart from gold, people came; although they are described as 'peaceable'. That it is assumed most people by the end of the 19th century were totally ignorant of this history is also an interesting feature of the story.

Interestingly in the first years of the twentieth century a number of reminiscences by elderly people of Robe and the Chinese arrivals were published. While the numbers of Chinese gold seeker arrivals are given and the poll tax is mentioned, the word 'invasion' never is, nor are accounts of false guides or people being pushed overboard.[498] It is not until 1925 that you begin to get an account that feels the need to make the straight history more dramatic. In an article pointedly entitled 'Romance of Early Robe' the Chinese gold seekers aspect of the story is simply squeezed in along with 'Wrecks and wreckers, Chinamen, soldiers, vice-royalty, poets, and keen political struggles'. No invasion or other drama, just an addition to the excitement in passing, mostly associated with their being passengers on various shipwrecks.[499] Robe around this time began to be seen as a holiday destination and so the need to add a little more excitement to its now 'picturesque' history seems to have become irresistible. A 1928 account of Robe's 'Glorious Coastline and Historic Places' begins modestly with the remark that many 'unfortunate Celestials never reached their destination'.[500] The desire for history over drama was not yet dead however, and the same year saw an article appear using extensive newspaper research to give what was perhaps the first detailed history of the Robe Walk. Based as it is on contemporary newspaper reports the most dramatic element it contains is an allusion to 'the ill-treatment of Chinese at Port Adelaide'. No invasion or deaths, just paid hospital admission.[501]

The first use of the term 'invasion' in the 20th century occurred in 1936 in an article headlined – 'CHINESE INVASION OF 80 YEARS AGO' – in which it is acknowledged that: 'The pursuance of the White Australia policy has rendered the Chinaman a curiosity in this State ...'[502] The account is accurate enough as far as numbers are concerned but repeats the false guides story before adding a previously unknown fear of daytime arrival, one that has the walkers 'creep into the fields under the cover of darkness' [503] This habit the Chinese Protector's regular journal and observations of the arrival of the Chinese walkers at the time never alludes to.

Other accounts begin to add such details as bones left 'rotting in the bush', being threatened with a 'hasty departure overboard' if the charge for being taken ashore was not agreed to, an early mention of Chinamans Wells, though not yet the assumption that they built it, and a repeat of the false guides story.[504] The death of old residents of Robe such as Mary Angell and Margaret Dening are also often noted, but the disappearance of these eye witnesses who never mentioned such details seems merely to allow free reign to those willing to keep adding to the drama of the accounts.[505]

The centenary of Robe as a port in 1946 seems to have inspired an effort to make Robe's history as exciting as possible but in general the Chinese arrivals are still only one part of the story told a little inaccurately as to dates but without invasion hysteria.[506] *The Chronicle* contributed a slight variation on its oft repeated account from the previous decade, this time it is an "Oriental Invasion" rather than a Chinese one.[507] Though accounts of the actual centenary celebrations at Robe scarcely mention the Chinese walkers at all.[508]

White Australia Policy - II

By the early 20th century, the White Australia Policy had not only reduced the numbers of Chinese people in Australia but had stimulated a 'whitewashing' of Australian history. A major impact of this was that the "Chinese" were increasingly seen as an exotic element within Australian history to be ignored or forgotten where possible or limited to goldmining or market gardening when not.✦ Thus, tales of large-scale organisation and legal challenges, along with opera performances and tobacco farms, and many other occupations outside of mining, cooking and gardening were

---

✦ Illustrative of this position at the height of the White Australia project is an entry in *The Australian Encyclopaedia* of 1925 where under 'Chinese in Australia' it simply says: 'See Immigration Restriction'.

not so much forgotten, as became inconceivable in this white construction of Australian history.♣

Paradoxically this ignorance and exoticism of the Chinese seems to have also contributed to their being assigned the origin of anything also perceived as exotic or of unknown origin. Thus, the Chinese imprint on Australia has been increased at the same time it was being washed away. As we have seen wells, not to mention cisterns, woolsheds, fancy fretwork, dams and stone walls have all been attributed to the work of mysterious Chinese craftsmen in western Victoria at least.

Why no academic study?

In all this mythologising and stereotyping academic historians have not played a very commendable role. Of course, the belief that one already knows something acts as a powerful barrier to improving one's knowledge. Australian historians have largely seen its Chinese elements as just that – side elements that give them little incentive not to repeat,

---

♣ For an examination of Chinese Opera in 19th and early 20th century Australia see, Michael Williams, "Smoking opium, puffing cigars, and drinking ginger beer: Chinese Opera in Australia", in *Opera, Emotion, and the Antipodes Volume II Applied Perspectives: Compositions and Performances*, edited by Jane W. Davidson, Michael Halliwell and Stephanie Rocke, pp.166-208. Abingdon: Routledge, 2020.

or at best subvert without demolishing, stereotypes. Far from examining these myths and striving to un-whitewash Australian history they have by and large indulged in only token efforts of reverse racism and have left it to historians of 'migrants' and 'ethnic' histories to build up parallel histories that have failed to impinge upon what is seen by default to be 'real' [white] Australian history.

Exoticism

This dealing with things "Chinese" in a vacuum lead to a host of strange conclusions. Luebbers for example develops a theory of 'tactical responses' 'along a well-known route' to explain Chinamans Well despite acknowledging it is a route well-travelled and scattered with wells. He imagines 'probable' masons on board ships 'assigned the task of installing water holes'. The single known well becoming 'a string of wells' and an attempt to build 'a cross-country network'. The fact that thousands of Chinese people in Victoria and NSW and later Queensland did nothing of the sort beyond their gold claims not causing pause because this kind of comparison with what is after all Australian history was not considered. Instead, the focus is kept narrow and thus fails to explain. In a similar fashion the Chinese walkers are often dumped on an entirely empty landscape despite the years of European travel across the same country. With European travel ignored Luebbers and the Chinese also apparently 'may have turned to Ngarrindjeri knowledge of local water supplies'.[509] Even when the archaeology is under review the exotic assumptions continue. Thus, the cutting of the round cap stones – readily recognised as standard millstone cutting techniques common in 19th century Britain, becomes an 'ancient technology' that is 'designed to last centuries under heavy use'.[510]

It is interesting to note that a survey undertaken just a couple of years prior to Luebbers makes no such assumptions and while mentioning the Chinese as builders of wells does not go so far as to assert anything. Instead, we have the comparatively modest statement: 'Although it is not known if the Chinese were responsible for the construction of the wells, it is likely that from the name Chinamans well, they had some particular association with that site.'[511] One wonders what Luebbers might have made of the well had his three Chinese archaeologists not been available for a picnic.

Robe itself helps perpetuate some of the misinformation that characterises this history in a panel display to be found in the Robe Customs House Museum. In a mostly not too inaccurate general overview of the poll tax and the numbers who walked from Robe there is a total confusion between the Amoy indentured and the Cantonese gold seekers and their very different ships and traveling circumstances. As well, the responsibility for the movement to Robe is placed on the ships captains as they 'rushed to carry the Chinese'. The absence of any knowledge of the credit-ticket system or the agents operating in Hong Kong to charter these ships is obvious.♦[512] Eric Rolls to his credit, despite his too ready acceptance of many implausibility's does point out that: 'Chinese miners not ship captains decided were they would disembark.'[513]

A more recent example of poor scholarship is Victorian Collections - *The Treks from Robe by Cash Brown*. This is obviously a cut and paste job repeating without question most of the stereotypes and myths. Yet because it is on a museums website it perpetuates these myths and even gives them greater credibility.[514]

♦ The myth of Mrs Brewer's death as a result of looking after sick Chinese gold seekers is also repeated here. See pp.169-170 above.

Parallel history

The general treatment of the history of the Robe Walk itself is an example of how Chinese Australian history is seen as a parallel rather than an integral part of Australian history. The Robe Walk has been celebrated as an element of Chinese Australian history as has the similar walk of (white) South Australians to the Victorian goldfields. Thus in 1985 the "16,000 men who left South Australia for the Victorian diggings in 1852-3" were celebrated in "The Tolmer Gold Escort re-enactment".[515] In 2010 a similar re-enactment took place conducted by Australians of Chinese heritage.[516] But are they not both part of the same history? As far as the accounts are concerned these two groups have literally marched parallel to each other on their way to the Victorian goldfields without ever meeting. In a sense this was how it was at the time given the psychological and cultural gulf, but should historians perpetuate this?

Post-White Australia policy

Over credulity regarding oral accounts, ignorance of culture and motivations, lack of context and a lingering perception of victimhood perhaps explain the local histories of the Robe Walk produced in the mid-20th century. However, they do not explain the persistence of these myths into the later 20th century and beyond. Here we see a remarkable set of circumstances which combines a trifecta of influences; white guilt, migrant progress, and a concept known as the '100 years of humiliation'.

White Guilt

Why do the general accounts of the Robe Walk emphasise hardship over organisation and ill treatment of Chinese gold seekers by others? There is a strong focus on the walkers as victims with only a stolid ability to bear hardship allowing them to survive at all. This set of stereotypes suited the anti-Chinese movement of the later 19th century.[517] Surprisingly it also suits the white guilt post-multiculturalists of the later 20th century, as well as recent immigrants of Chinese heritage, often imbued with the 100 years of humiliation trope, of the early 21st century.

The dismantling of the White Australia policy in the late 20th century and the growth of multiculturalism left the victim characterisation of the Chinese walkers relatively untouched. This was because the "white guilt" component of multiculturalism, while allowing for greater sympathy for "people of colour", continues to see "white" Australians at the centre of the historical stage, even or particularly when perpetrating outrages and discrimination. From this perspective there is no incentive to examine a Chinese walker's standpoint, instead the poll tax and the walk itself is simply acknowledged as a wrong that "whites" perpetrated and the rest of the story can remain intact. The gradual evolving of the less racist perspectives of a multicultural Australia is insufficient to rise above a view of Chinese people as hapless victims enduring great suffering. In fact, the white guilt generated by multicultural Australia stimulates the retelling of dramatic incidences of hardship and suffering at the hands of "bad" whites.[518]

Surprisingly the increasing number of Chinese Australians (either by heritage or recent migrants) who become interested in Chinese Australian history do not automatically adopt a "Chinese" standpoint. Instead, like those employing "white guilt" perspectives, they usually prefer to adopt an attitude of sympathy and outrage. The "migrant success" trope is a common one that can parallel white pioneer history whereby present success is to be explained and enjoyed on the basis of the endurance and suffering of forebears.♦

♦ Forebears real or imagined, with many northern and/or Mandarin speaking people of China ignoring the Cantonese or southern origins of nearly all Chinese Australians before the 1980s. Rather like the English

Victimhood and lack of agency are acceptable in contrast to contemporary agency and equality. This perspective again provides no incentive to look past the victim narrative.

For many Australians of Chinese heritage this perspective is further reenforced by the political attacks on China as a nation and the fact that many will have been educated in what is called the "100 years of humiliation" trope.[519] This refers to the 100 years from roughly 1849 to 1949 or from the First Opium War to the advent of the People's Republic of China. Within this perspective racism and discrimination against Chinese people around the world, including of course Australia, is seen as unrelenting and overwhelming. This is a humiliation, so the trope goes, only ended with strong (Communist Party) government in China. Many new migrants from China would have been educated in his version of history and so would also readily accept the Robe Walk history as it is presented in all its most extreme forms without nuance or agency.

---

ignoring the Scots origins of an historical group and claiming kinship as all British.

Conclusion

(12) Wrapping up – parallel histories & a new generation of myths

In 2023 an ABC report once again told the "hidden" history of how as a result of the Victorian poll tax and ship passenger limit it was on the initiative of ship captains that Chinese gold seekers were suddenly dumped at Robe and left to walk the extra distance as best they could. The journalist largely accepted the story from a local Bendigo self-appointed expert in the absence of any obvious contrary account. As we have seen here, the planning that originated in Hong Kong very soon after the new laws were known, the nature of how ships were chartered, and the shift to Robe after only a year of using Adelaide as the alternative port alone makes nonsense of any such impressions.

It is an irony of historical research that it was probably well publicised court cases such as that involving Ayun discussed above that may have inspired the impression ship captains were in control. For of course this case actually demonstrates the opposite. As does the detailed journal kept by Foster when his yearlong failure to observe sickness or extreme hardship is subverted by quoting out of context his one observation of a brief period when this was not the case. In a lack of context, the exception to the rule becomes the rule.

Far from being a desperate bid to escape an unjust law leading to heroic measures, the walk from Robe was a measured effort to continue previous patterns and avoid a certainly unjust but relatively minor legal impediment. Heroics there may well have been but like the majority of heroics performed by the everyday individual they are unrecorded by history. Why there is an apparent need for heroics is the more interesting question as the role of Chinese people in Australian history continues to be re-examined and re-evaluated in the eyes of the present.

Is there a solution to this historical problem? Certainly, there is a need to integrate this history within the wider scope of Australian and not merely a parallel "ethnic" history. This is a need to recognise and overcome the trifecta of white guilt, migrant exceptionalism and 100 years of humiliation. It would also assist in subverting the contemporary "fear of China" narrative that threatens to add a fourth dimension to an already overcrowded list of ahistorical perceptions. This would see the Robe walkers as part of the global movement of gold seekers arriving in Australia, not the same in all respects but not so different either. That they were treated differently can then be seen as part of the race-based sense of identity the Australian colonies were developing. A cherry picking emphasis on the victimhood and aggressions of the white population are all about maintaining the agency and centrality of "white" Australian history. The agency and control of Chinese people as shown in the planned and well mounted strategies of the gold seekers is unsettling and difficult to comprehend. Time for Australian historians to move on from their white supremacy – positive or negative – perspective.

Given the scale and distances involved it is remarkable that the vast majority arrived where they intended with relatively few sufferings unduly. In other words, the Chinese in Australia, despite discriminatory laws, being treated as foreigners, and with great language and cultural barriers did very much what they set out to do. That is, the Chinese not the Europeans are the centre of this history despite the best efforts of European Australian historians and their partner mythmakers to make it otherwise.◆

◆ For a detailed analysis of this Chinese centred context see Williams, *Returning Home with Glory*.

Thus, it can be seen that a near perfect storm of factors would lead to a continuation of what I would nevertheless describe as the Robe Walk myth with its emphasis on lack of agency and victimhood. The history presented here does not seek to minimise or deny the hardship of the Robe trek including the many instances of discrimination and oppression that undoubtedly occurred, not to mention the racist legislation that necessitated the switch in routes to the goldfields in the first place. But it does seek to show that far from lacking agency the 16,000 odd gold seekers from the Pearl River Delta were well organised and well looked after in the main. They knew what they wanted and how to achieve it despite discriminatory laws, racism and unfair practices, and they arrived armed with every requisite for the hardships they met and having done so largely achieved what they set out to do. This is a story integral to Australian history, not parallel to it.

References

Newspapers

The Adelaide Chronicle
Adelaide Observer
Adelaide Times
The Age
The Argus
Bell's Life in Victoria and Sporting Chronicle
Bendigo Advertiser
Border Watch
Burra Record
The Cornwall Chronicle
The Courier
The Empire
Freeman's Journal
Geelong Advertiser
Hamilton Spectator and Grange District Advertiser
The Herald
Hobarton Guardian, or, True Friend of Tasmania
Launceston Examiner
The Leader
The Maitland Mercury and Hunter River General Advertiser
The Mercury
Mount Alexander Mail
Narracoorte Herald
News
Ovens and Murray Advertiser
Portland Guardian and Normanby General Advertiser
Quiz and the Lantern
The Shipping Gazette and Sydney General Trade List

South Australian Register
South Australian Record and Australasian Chronicle
South Australian Weekly Chronicle
The Star
The Sydney Morning Herald
The Tasmanian Colonist

Archives

Admission papers, Colonial Lunatic Asylum, 1858 unnumbered, John Chinaman, State Records SA: GRS 13461/00001.

Brewer, John, 1838-1914, Reminiscences of John Brewer (Notes written in 1968 by John L. Cantrill/Cantrell), State Library of South Australia, D Piece (Archival), D 7378(L).

Campbell, Roland, Letter to Mr Smith, Kingston, 18 May 1941, Millicent, State Library of South Australia, PRG 497.

'Chinese at Coleraine', Coleraine Historical Society file document, 2017.

Despatches from the Governor of South Australia to the Secretary of State for the Colonies, from 9th December 1853, to 31st December 1855, State Records SA: GRG2, 6/00000.

Ewens, John Reynolds, 1835-1888, Private journal of J. R. Ewens, Police trooper, 1853-1862, State Library of South Australia, D 8334 (L).

Foster, W.H., *Letter book, Reports and Diary, Ballarat*, September 1855 to December 1859, Victorian Public Records, S751.

Guichen Bay Police Station Records, 1851 – 1863, State Records SA: GRG5/159.

Melville, Henry Dudley, 'Compensation for A Life's Service under Civil Service Regulations of South

Australia 1887', Reminiscences of H D Melville, Volume 2, 1887, State Library of South Australia, D6976/2 (L).

Smeaton, Thomas Dury, *Our Invasion by Chinese*, 1865, State Library of South Australia Research Notes RN 830.

Verco, Joseph Cooke - Records, 1851 - 1924, State Library of South Australia, PRG 322/6.

Primary

Bonwick, James, *Western Victoria, Its Geography, Geology, and Social Condition; the Narrative of an Educational Tour in 1857*. With an Introduction and Editorial Commentary by C. E. Sayers, Heinemann, 1970.

Burr, Thomas. and Grey, G. "Account of Governor G. Grey's Exploratory Journey along the South-Eastern Sea-Board of South Australia." *The Journal of the Royal Geographical Society of London* 15 (1845), pp.160–84.

Chandler, J. *Forty Years in the Wilderness*, E. Wyatt, Printer, 1893.

CORRESPONDENCE relative to the conveyance of CHINESE IMMIGRANTS into VICTORIA by steamers, via the RIVER MURRAY. Ordered by the Legislative Council to be printed, May 6th, 1857.

Duffy, Charles Gavan (& Louis Ah Mouy?), *The Chinese Question Analyzed; with a Full Statement of Facts: by One Who Knows Them*, Steam Press of W. Fairfax & Co., 1857.

Fetherstonhaugh, Cuthbert, and Ian J. Itter. *After Many Days (Revisited): Being the Reminiscenes of Cuthbert Fetherstonhaugh*; Swan Hill, Vic.: I. Itter, 2012.

Ragless, Oliver & Ragless, Margaret E, *Oliver's diary: an 'andkichef of eirth [sic]*. Investigator Press, Hawthorndene, S. Australia, 1986.

Woods, Julian Tenison, Ten Years in the Bush, *The Australasian Catholic Record*, July 1989, pp.259-278.

Williams's Melbourne almanac 1858, Melbourne: George Slater, 1858.

Williams, Michael, Personal interactions in around Robe, South Australia and the western districts of Victoria, April 2022.

Secondary

Baker, Ronald & Margaret., *Coorong pilot: lower Murray lakes and Coorong, South Australia*, Adelaide, Fullers Services, 1978.

Barrowman, Alexander Hutchison, *Old days and old ways*, Robe, S. Aust., A. H. Barrowman, 1971.

Blake, L. J. *Gold Escort*, Hawthorn Press, 1971.

Cawthorne, Ellen Mary, *The Long Journey: The Story of the Chinese Landings at Robe during the Gold Rush Era, 1852-63*, Hansen House, S.A., 1974.

Clark, Ian D., *Aboriginal Languages and Clans: An Historical Atlas of Western and Central Victoria, 1800-1900* / Dept. of Geography and Environmental Science, Monash University, 1990.

Cronin, Kathryn, *Colonial casualties: Chinese in early Victoria*, Melbourne University Press Melbourne, 1982.

Darnell, Maxine, "Responses and Reactions to the Importation of Indentured Chinese Labourers", Working Paper Series in Economic History, No.99-2, November 1999, pp1-24.

Edwards, Louise, "Victims, Apologies, and the Chinese in Australia", *Journal of Chinese Overseas*, 15 (1), pp.62-88, 2019.

Edwards, Robert, "Chinese coins from an Aboriginal camp-site on the Coorong, South Australia", *Australian Numismatic Journal*, Vol.17, No.3, July-Sept, 1966, pp.102-105.

Fitzgerald John, "China's 'Century of Humiliation' and Chinese-Australian History", *Chinese Southern Diaspora Studies*, Volume Eight, 2019, pp.230-235.

Golden Dragon Museum, *The Walk from Robe*, Bendigo Chinese Association Museum, 2001.

Harfull, Liz, *Guichen Bay and the Chinese Landings*, District Council of Robe, 2017.

Heritage Council of New South Wales, and Hughes, Trueman, Ludlow, *Wells and Underground Tanks*, Heritage Council of New South Wales, 1984.

Horsfall, David, *March to Big Gold Mountain*, Red Rooster Press, 1985.

Hubbard, Timothy, *Mount Sturgeon's 'Chinese' Wall: A Planning Report on its Significance*, Heritage Matters, Port Fairy, Victoria, 2018.

Jeffery, Bill and Kenderdine, Sarah, "Chinese Emigration to South Australia aboard Foreign-owned Vessels: The Guichen Bay Shipwrecks of 1857", *The Bulletin of the Australian Institute for Maritime Archaeology* 15.1 (1991): 31-36.

Jenkin, Graham, *Conquest of the Ngarrindjeri*, Adelaide: Rigby, 1979.

Kirkman, Noreen, 'Chinese Miners on the Palmer', *Journal of the Royal Historical Society of Queensland*, vol. 13, no. 2, 1987.

Kyi, Anna, '"The most determined, sustained diggers' resistance campaign": Chinese protests against the Victorian Government's anti-Chinese legislation 1855-1862', *Provenance: The Journal of Public Record Office Victoria*, Issue No. 8, 2009.

Lindsay, H.A., "Who Did Build the Chinaman's Well?", *Sunday Mail*, 23 October 1965, p.44.

Lindsay, H.A., "Mystery of Well", *Sunday Mail*, 30 October 1965, p.x.

Loh, Morag, *Sojourners and Settlers, Chinese in Victoria, 1848-1985*, Victorian Government China Advisory Committee, 1985.

Loy-Wilson, Sophie, "Coolie alibis: Seizing gold from Chinese miners in New South Wales," *International Labor and Working Class History*, 91, 2017.

Luebbers, Roger, *Recommendations for the Management of the Cultural Heritage of Chinamans Wells, Coorong National Park*, report to Department of Environment & Planning, Adelaide, 1984.

Luebbers, Roger, *The Archaeology of Chinamans Wells and Hacks Station, The Coorong, South Australia*, report to Department of Environment & Natural Resources, Adelaide, 1995.

McAlpine, R. A., *The Shire of Hampden, 1863-1963*, Hampden Shire Council, 1963.

McCalman, Janet, *Vandemonians: The Repressed History of Colonial Victoria* (Melbourne University Press, 2021.

McGowan, Barry, "Reconsidering race: The Chinese experience on the goldfields of southern New South Wales", *Australian Historical Studies*, October 2004, Vol.36 (124), p.312-331.

Memmott, Paul, *Gunyah, Goondie and Wurley: the Aboriginal architecture of Australia*, St Lucia, University of Queensland Press, 2007.

Miles, Steven B, *Opportunity in Crisis: Cantonese Migrants and the State in Late Qing China*, Harvard East Asian Monographs, 2021.

Moloney, David, Rowe, David, Jellie, Pamela, "Former Robinson Water Tank, The Bullock Track", *Shire of Melton Heritage Study, Volume 5*, 2006.

Moodie, William, *William Moodie: a Pioneer of Western Victoria*, Victoria: Hedges and Bell, 1973.

Munday, Bruce, *Those dry-stone walls: stories from South Australia's stone age*, Wakefield Press, 2012.

National Parks South Australia, *Coorong National Park, Coorong Self-guided History Trail*, 2020?
https://cdn.environment.sa.gov.au/parks/docs/coorong-national-park/coorong-self-guided-history-trail.pdf

Parsons, Ronald, *Australian coastal passenger ships: the details and a brief outline of the career of every steam* and motor ship that carried passengers on the Australian coast, Ronald H. Parsons, Magill, SA, 1981.

Parsons, Ronald, *Southern passages: a maritime history of South Australia*, Netley, S. Aust.: Wakefield Press, 1986.

Paton, Penny, 'Chinamans Well' in Paton, D. C., *At the end of the river: the Coorong and lower lakes*, ATF Press, Hindmarsh, SA, 2010.

Rendell, M.P. 'The Chinese in South Australia before 1860'. *Proceedings of the Royal Geographical Society of Australasia, South Australian Branch*, vol.54, 1953, pp.22-33.

Ritchie, Fiona, *Guichen Bay to Canton Lead: The Chinese Trek to Gold*, District Council of Robe, 2004.

Rolls, Eric, *Sojourners: Flowers and the Wide Sea*, University of Queensland Press, 1992.

Rolls, Eric, *Citizens: Flowers and the Wide Sea*, University of Queensland Press, 1996.

Rudduck, Penny, *European Heritage of the Coorong: A general survey of the sites of Early European Heritage of the area now comprising the Coorong National Park and Coorong Game Reserve*, National Parks and Wildlife Service. May, 1982.

Schamberger Karen, "The Lambing Flat Riots and Its Legacies 1861-2021", Young Historical Museum, July 2021, https://younghistoricalmuseum.wordpress.com/2021/07/15/the-lambing-flat-riots-and-its-legacies-1861-2021/

Seebeck, J. H., "Mammals of the plains or, where have all the wombats gone?", in Conley, D. N., et al. *The Western Plains, a Natural and Social History: Papers from the Symposium October 8th and 9th 1983*, Australian Institute of Agricultural Science, 1984, pp.39-53.

Sharp, Eloise I., *E.T. Hooley, Pioneer Bushman: Stock Route Pioneered by E.T. Hooley from Geraldine Mine to Nicol Bay, 1866, and 1905 Government Wells*, E.I. Sharp, 1985.

Snoek, W., *Archaeological report of Chinamans Wells, the Coorong National Park*, South Australian Department of Environment and Planning, 1984.

Sprengel, Wilf, *Robe's Chinese invasion, 1857-1863*, Narracoorte, Hansen Print, 1986.

Stanin, Z., "From Li Chun to Yong Kit: a market garden on the Loddon, 1851-1912", Paper in special issue: Active Voices, Hidden Histories: The Chinese in Colonial Australia, *Journal of Australian Colonial History*, 6 (2004), pp.14–34.

Wang Sing-wu, *The Organisation of Chinese Emigration 1848-1888: with special reference to Chinese Emigration to Australia* (San Francisco: Chinese Materials Centre, 1978).

Wong, J.Y., *Deadly Dreams: Opium and the Arrow War (1856–1860) in China*, Cambridge University Press, 1998.

Williams, Michael, 'Observations of a China Consul', *Locality*, Vol. 11, no.2, 2000, pp.24-31.

Williams, Michael, *Returning Home with Glory*, University of Hong Kong Press, 2019.

Williams, Michael, "Smoking opium, puffing cigars, and drinking ginger beer: Chinese Opera in Australia", in *Opera, Emotion, and the Antipodes Volume II Applied Perspectives: Compositions and Performances*, edited by Jane W. Davidson, Michael Halliwell and Stephanie Rocke, pp.166-208. Abingdon: Routledge, 2020.

Williams, Michael, *Australia's Dictation Test: The Test it was a Crime to Fail*, Brill, 2021.

Williams, Michael, 'Vegetables varied and excellent, chiefly from a Celestial Garden', *History*, September 2022, pp.9-11.

Williams, Michael, 'Villages of the Fragrant Hills' in *Heritage and History in the China-Australia Migration Corridor*, University of Hong Kong Press, 2023, pp.25-51.

Wu, Rebecca, "Oz Asia Review: The Long Walk", *Glam Adelaide*, posted October 26, 2022.

Unpublished
Ararat Chinese Heritage Society, *Chinese and the ships to Adelaide 1856*, Research Report 1998.
Cash, Damien, The Convicts Prevention Act in Victoria, 1852-1856, Honours thesis, University of Melbourne, 1978.
Copland, Gordon Arthur, *Event driven transitory migration the case of the Chinese migration through South Australia between 1854 and 1864*, Honours Thesis, Finders University, 1998.
Dean, Lois, *Speech by Lois Dean at Chinese Gold seekers seminar 8th June 1996 as part of Robe's 150 Celebrations*, Robe Historical Society, 1996.
Dunkeld and District Historical Museum, *Transcribing and Editing of audio tape of Monthly meeting held on 5th November, 1990 – The Chinese Invasion.*

Websites
State Library of Queensland
  https://www.slq.qld.gov.au/blog/chinese-business-history-queensland-gold-rush-1851-1881
Sydney Living Museums
  https://sydneylivingmuseums.com.au/stories/chinese-goldfields
Victorian Collections,
  Many Roads: Stories of the Chinese on the goldfields,
  https://victoriancollections.net.au/stories/many-roads-stories-of-the-chinese-on-the-goldfields
  The Treks from Robe by Cash Brown,
  https://victoriancollections.net.au/media/exhibitions/5fbd874fd5fa8108043fc293//5fc8d9e89992142684f04d6a/original.pdf
Walking South Australia, *Chinaman's Well Historic Site Journey to Gold Walk*, 2020?
  https://www.walkingsa.org.au/walk/find-a-place-to-walk/chinamans-well-historic-site-journey-to-gold-walk-coorong-national-park/

Acknowledgements

All research is dependent on the assistance and generosity of others and not only is this work no exception but it is perhaps more reliant than many. Certainly, thanks are due to Alison Wong whose suggestion we retrace the footsteps of the walkers it was and who perseverance made it happen. I wish her well in her own project also to be based on our walk. Alongside Alison was her husband Kevin who generously drove us to and from our walking spots along the lonely roads of western Victoria. My own spouse Mei-Su Chen is a constant support in all my research and in this instance accompanied us part of the way. Much is due to my wife in thanks and appreciation always, as she often reminds me.

Along the way an amazing number of helpful locals and interested researchers provided their ideas, knowledge and suggestions. All were of great value in assisting the research and helping to avoid errors or wasting always limited time. Roger Andre showed us much of interest around his family lands between Robe and Penola and his local historical knowledge was invaluable. Liz Hartful is an outstanding historian and one of great generosity who happily shared all she had from her own researches. Something not all historians are a willing to do as you might hope. Valerie Monaghan in Robe was equally generous and constantly made helpful suggestions that was of much assistance.

The number of generous locals of the western districts of Victoria are too numerous to mention but two who must be named are Ely Finch who provided us with a lovely lunch and much useful information as is his usual wont. Also of great assistance was Allan Murray Sambell who unstintingly shared his family artifact.

Woolshed owners, historical society volunteers, heritage researchers, stonemasons, archivists, librarians and many more make up the host of generous people's that assisted with this research in so many ways. As usual only I however am responsible for any errors that may appear.

Image 26: The author researching

Author Bio

Michael Williams is a graduate of Hong Kong University, a scholar of Chinese-Australian history and a founding member of the Chinese-Australian Historical Society. He is the author of *Returning Home with Glory*, HKU Press, 2018, which traces the history of peoples from south China's Pearl River Delta around the Pacific Ports of Sydney, Hawaii and San Francisco. Michael has taught at Beijing Foreign Studies and Peking Universities and is formerly an Adjunct Professor at the Institute for Australian and Chinese Arts and Culture (IAC), Western Sydney University. His website: Chinese Australian History in 88 Objects was shortlisted for the 2022 Premiers Digital History Prize and his most recent book before this was *Australia's Dictation Test: The Test it was a Crime to Fail*, Brill, 2021. Michael is currently developing a national database of Chinese Australian history called: *Scattered Legacy* / 澳華僑海集珍.

Endnotes

Introduction

[1] According to one account it "must be one of the epic events of Australian history", Horsfall, David, *March to Big Gold Mountain*, Red Rooster Press, 1985, p.1. And more recently a dance event in Adelaide called it "The Long Walk", Rebecca Wu, "Oz Asia Review: The Long Walk", *Glam Adelaide*, posted October 26, 2022.

[2] Examples are: Ellen Mary Cawthorne, *The Long Journey: The Story of the Chinese Landings at Robe during the Gold Rush Era, 1852-63*, Hansen House, S.A., 1974; Wilf Sprengel, *Robe's Chinese invasion, 1857-1863*, Narracoorte, Hansen Print, 1986; Golden Dragon Museum, *The Walk from Robe*, Bendigo Chinese Association Museum, 2001; Fiona Ritchie, *Guichen Bay to Canton Lead: The Chinese Trek to Gold*, District Council of Robe, 2004. Most recent is Liz Harfull, *Guichen Bay and the Chinese Landings*, District Council of Robe, 2017, a decided improvement but focused on Robe only. The two exceptions to the dearth of academic studies are Margret Rendell, 'The Chinese in South Australia before 1860', *Proceedings of the Royal Geographical Society of Australasia, South Australian Branch*, vol.54, 1953, pp.22-33 & Gordon Copland, *Event driven transitory migration the case of the Chinese migration through South Australia between 1854 and 1864*, Honours Thesis, Finders University, 1998. Perhaps the fact that Rendell's is a largely straightforward account, nearly devoid of reference to the usual exaggerations and myths, and describing the history as merely having 'a certain interest in itself', explains its near absence as a source.

[3] Even before arrival according to Sprengel, *Robe's Chinese invasion*, p.4.

Chapter 1

[4] In 1854 there were 17,000 Chinese people in California and 18,000 in Victoria in 1855, Michael Williams, *Returning Home with Glory*, University of Hong Kong Press, 2019, pp.50-51.

[5] "[T]hey [Chinese] are not much better than ... Vandemonians", *The Argus*, 15 July 1856, p.6. For the Convicts' Prevention Act, see Janet McCalman, *Vandemonians: The Repressed History of Colonial Victoria* (Melbourne University Press, 2021), p.112.

[6] *The Argus*, 2 June 1855, p.4.

[7] This was: *An Act - To make provision for certain Immigrants*, No.2, 1855.

[8] *The Argus*, 25 July 1856, p.6.

[9] *Mount Alexander Mail*, 8 June 1855, p.3.

[10] For an account that explains clearly the difference between indenture and credit-ticket see, Wang Sing-wu, *The Organisation of Chinese Emigration 1848-1888: with special reference to Chinese Emigration to Australia* (San Francisco: Chinese Materials Centre, 1978).

[11] *An Act - To make provision for certain Immigrants*, No.2, 1855.

[12] *South Australian Register*, 3 June 1856, p.3.

[13] *Adelaide Times*, 25 August 1857, p.1. Puzzling is a Melbourne to Portland steamer advert which makes a similar claim though the distance overland from either Melbourne or Portland to the goldfields is nearly the same. See, *The Argus*, 19 November 1857, p.1.

[14] *South Australian Register*, 6 November 1847, p.2.

[15] *The Maitland Mercury and Hunter River General Advertiser*, 22 March 1851, p.2. See also, Ronald Parsons, *Australian coastal passenger ships: the details and a brief outline of the career of every steam and motor ship that carried passengers on the Australian coast*, Ronald H. Parsons, Magill, SA, 1981.

[16] *The Age*, 28 August 1857, p.4.

[17] *Empire*, 6 February 1857, p.2.

[18] *Adelaide Observer*, 16 May 1857, p.6.

[19] *Despatch No.186, to Secretary of State for Colonies*, Government House, Adelaide, 15 October 1857.

[20] Ararat Chinese Heritage Society, *Chinese and the ships to Adelaide 1856*, Research Report 1998.

[21] *South Australian Register*, 22 January 1856, p.3.

[22] *Adelaide Observer*, 7 February 1857, p.8.

[23] *No. 3: An Act to make provision for levying a charge on Chinese arriving in South Australia.* [Assented to, 19th November, 1857.]

First introduced in June (*The Maitland Mercury and Hunter River General Advertiser*, 27 June 1857, p.6), it began operating from 1st December, 1857.

[24] *No. 14. An Act to repeal An Act, No. 3 of 1857-8, intituled "An Act to make provision for levying a charge on Chinese arriving in South Australia.* [Assented to, 29th November, 1861.]

Chapter 2

[25] Steven B Miles, *Opportunity in Crisis: Cantonese Migrants and the State in Late Qing China*, Harvard East Asian Monographs, 2021, p.14. For more details see also, Williams, *Returning Home with Glory*, pp.47-51.

[26] *South Australian Register*, 26 November 1845, p.3; Rendell, M.P. 'The Chinese in South Australia before 1860'. *Proceedings of the Royal Geographical Society of Australasia, South Australian Branch*, vol.54, 1953, p.24; *Hamilton Spectator*, 6 August 1896, p.3; *Adelaide Observer*, 14 May 1853, p.6; *The Tasmanian Colonist*, 16 March 1854, p.4; *South Australian Register*, 21 September 1855, p.3; *South Australian Register*, 31 December 1855, p.3; *Geelong Advertiser and Intelligencer*, 29 March 1856, p.2; *Adelaide Times*, 15 October 1856, p.2.

[27] *South Australian Register*, 2 October 1858, p.3.

[28] For more on the Amoy men see Maxine Darnell, "Responses and Reactions to the Importation of Indentured Chinese Labourers", Working Paper Series in Economic History, No.99-2, November 1999, pp.1-24.

[29] Sprengel, *Robe's Chinese invasion*, p.6, is not unusual in failing to recognise any distinction between people of Fujian and those of Canton.

[30] *Adelaide Times*, 24 March 1857, p.3.

[31] *The Argus*, 26 January 1857, p.5.

[32] *South Australian Register*, 11 June 1854, p.4.

[33] Despatch No. 198, to Secretary of State for Colonies, Government House, Adelaide, 26 November 1857.

[34] *South Australian Register*, 16 March 1852, p.3.

[35] *South Australian Register*, 27 March 1857, p.3.

[36] *South Australian Register*, 16 March 1852, p.3.

[37] Ragless, Oliver & Ragless, Margaret E, *Oliver's diary: an 'andkichef of eirth [sic]*. Investigator Press, Hawthorndene, S. Australia, 1986, pp.17-18.

[38] *South Australian Register*, 11 June 1856, p.4.

[39] *South Australian Register*, 26 March 1852, p.3.

[40] *Hobarton Guardian, or, True Friend of Tasmania*, 17 April 1852, p.3.
[41] *South Australian Register*, 13 April 1852, p.3.
[42] *The Star*, 20 August 1857, p.2.
[43] *Adelaide Times*, 10 March 1856, p.2.
[44] Kirkman, Noreen, 'Chinese Miners on the Palmer', *Journal of the Royal Historical Society of Queensland*, vol. 13, no. 2, 1987, pp.49-62.
[45] *Adelaide Times*, 5 March 1856, p.3.
[46] All these aspects of the Chinese gold seekers are discussed below.
[47] *Geelong Advertiser*, 4 September 1862, p.2.
[48] For examples of such accounts see Victorian Collections, 'Fleeing violence, famine and poverty' [https://victoriancollections.net.au/stories/many-roads-stories-of-the-chinese-on-the-goldfields]; Sydney Living Museums, 'war, political instability and environmental conditions' [https://sydneylivingmuseums.com.au/stories/chinese-goldfields] and the State Library of Queensland, 'radical political and religious upheaval' [https://www.slq.qld.gov.au/blog/chinese-business-history-queensland-gold-rush-1851-1881].
[49] For an account of this perspective see Sophie Loy-Wilson, "Coolie alibis: Seizing gold from Chinese miners in New South Wales," *International Labor and Working Class History,* 91 (2017): pp.28–45.
[50] *The Argus*, 8 October 1857, p.5.
[51] *The Hobart Town Courier*, 5 March 1831, p.4.
[52] *The Star*, 4 August 1857, p.3.
[53] *Geelong Advertiser*, 4 September 1862, p.2.
[54] *The Sydney Morning Herald*, 29 April 1856, p.4.
[55] For example, *Adelaide Times,* 17 April 1856, p.2.
[56] Duffy, Charles Gavan (& Louis Ah Mouy?), *The Chinese Question Analyzed; with a Full Statement of Facts: by One Who Knows Them*, Steam Press of W. Fairfax & Co., 1857, p.13.
[57] *The Argus*, 26 August 1857, p.4.
[58] For more on this see, "Villages of the Fragrant Hills", pp.25-51, in *Heritage and History in the China-Australia Migration Corridor* (HKU Press, 2023).
[59] For a detailed account of this conflict see, J. Y. Wong, *Deadly Dreams: Opium and the Arrow War (1856–1860) in China*, Cambridge University Press, 1998.
[60] *Adelaide Times*, 24 March 1857, p.3.
[61] *South Australian Register*, 18 March 1857, p.2.
[62] *Adelaide Times*, 16 April 1855, p.3, referring to Melbourne, Victoria.

[63] W.H. Foster, *Letter book, Reports and Diary, Ballarat,* February 29th 1856, p.37, Victorian Public Records S751.
[64] Julian Tenison Woods, Ten Years in the Bush, *The Australasian Catholic Record*, July 1989, pp.264-265.

Chapter 3

[65] *Adelaide Times*, 16 April 1855, p.3.
[66] *South Australian Register*, 24 January 1856, p.3. See also a similar description at Bathurst, *Bathurst Free Press and Mining Journal*, 30 July 1856, p.2.
[67] For details of all these see, Williams, *Returning Home with Glory*, p.51.
[68] *The Argus*, 7 June 1855, p.5 & *The Argus*, 16 June 1855, p.6.
[69] *Adelaide Observer*, 29 September 1855, p.5 & *Mount Alexander Mail*, 5 October 1855, p.2.
[70] *Adelaide Times*, 23 January 1856, p.2.
[71] *South Australian Register*, 22 January 1856, p.3.
[72] *Bendigo Advertiser*, 28 September 1857, p.2.
[73] Foster, *Letter book*, February 29th 1856, p.37.
[74] *South Australian Register*, 24 January 1856, p.3.
[75] *South Australian Register*, 25 January 1856, p.2; *Adelaide Times*, 25 February 1856, p.3 & *The Age*, 20 August 1856, p.3.
[76] *Weekly Times*, 16 October 1920, p.29. *The Cornwall Chronicle*, 13 December 1856, p.4.
[77] *The Age*, 20 August 1856, p.3.
[78] *Adelaide Times*, 24 January 1856, p.2.
[79] *South Australian Register*, 1 October 1855, p.2.
[80] *South Australian Register*, 18 October 1855, p.2. For the *Havilah* see, Ronald Parsons, *Southern passages: a maritime history of South Australia*, Netley, S. Aust.: Wakefield Press, 1986, p.52.
[81] *Adelaide Observer*, 14 June 1856, p.3.
[82] *Adelaide Observer*, 31 December 1853, p.4.
[83] *South Australian Register*, 21 December 1855, p.2 & *South Australian Register*, 11 February 1856, p.2.
[84] *South Australian Register*, 13 April 1852, p.3.
[85] *South Australian Register*, 12 February 1856, p.3.
[86] *Adelaide Times*, 24 March 1856, p.3.
[87] *Adelaide Observer*, 21 June 1856, p.3.
[88] *Adelaide Observer*, 21 June 1856, p.3.
[89] *Adelaide Times*, 16 June 1856, p.2.
[90] *Adelaide Observer*, 21 June 1856, p.3.
[91] *The Argus*, 30 August 1856, p.5 & *The Age*, 30 August 1856, p.3.

[92] *The Argus*, 30 August 1856, p.5 & *The Age*, 30 August 1856, p.3.
[93] *The Argus*, 30 August 1856, p.5 & *The Age*, 30 August 1856, p.3.
[94] *The Argus*, 25 July 1856, p.6.
[95] *The Argus*, 30 August 1856, p.5 & *The Age*, 30 August 1856, p.3.
[96] *Adelaide Observer*, 5 July 1856, p.4.
[97] *The Argus*, 8 October 1857, p.5.
[98] *The Star*, 14 August 1857, p.3.
[99] *The Argus*, 7 August 1857, p.6.
[100] Chu a Luk to Barkly, 3 August 1857, forwarded to Chief Sec. in-letter A5948 of 1857, box 666: 'Chinese Petition', P.P. (Vic., L.A.) 1856-7; Stuart to Chief Sec., 27 May 1857, in-letter B5772, box 666. Quoted in Cronin, Kathryn, *Colonial casualties: Chinese in early Victoria*, Melbourne University Press, 1982, p.49.

Chapter 4

[101] *South Australian Register*, 7 June 1856, p.3.
[102] *Adelaide Observer*, 24 May 1856, p.8.
[103] *Adelaide Observer*, 19 July 1856, p.3.
[104] *Adelaide Times*, 3 June 1856, p.3 & *South Australian Register*, 15 January, 1853, p.3, 16 March 1852, p.3 & 5 May 1852, p.3
[105] *Adelaide Observer*, 3 April 1852, p.2 & *South Australian Register*, 16 March 1852, p.3.
[106] *South Australian Register*, 8 April 1856, p.3.
[107] *South Australian Register*, 4 June 1856, p.2.
[108] See Broadbent route, image 5.
[109] *South Australian Register*, 31 January 1852, p.3.
[110] For example, *South Australian Register*, 23 April 1856, p.2, 'The steamer *Young Australian*, 144 tons, for Guichen Bay. Passengers—250 Chinese.' & *South Australian Register*, 5 June 1856, p.2, 'The schooner *Fame* ... 101 Chinese.' 'The schooner *Daphne* ... 105 Chinese.' 'This day the Steamer Burra Burra arrived with 130 Chinese on their way to the diggins in Victoria.' State Records SA: GRG5/159, Guichen Bay Police Station Records 1851 – 1863, 2nd March 1856.
[111] *Bendigo Advertiser*, 20 May 1857, p.2.
[112] *Adelaide Times*, 24 March 1857, p.3.
[113] *Launceston Examiner*, 30 June 1857, p.2.
[114] *The Herald*, 5 September 1862, p.6.
[115] *Adelaide Times*, 9 June 1856, p.3. *Empire*, 20 November 1856, p.6.
[116] James Bonwick, *Western Victoria, Its Geography, Geology, and Social Condition; the Narrative of an Educational Tour in 1857*, Heinemann, 1970, p.158.

[117] *South Australian Register*, 16 March 1852, p.3.
[118] Mary MacKillop Penola Centre, Father Woods compass signage, quoting Father Woods.
[119] *South Australian Register*, 3 June 1857, p.3.
[120] *South Australian Register*, 16 March 1852, p.3.
[121] *South Australian Register*, 27 February 1856, p.2.
[122] Bonwick, *Western Victoria, Its Geography, Geology, and Social Condition*, p.126.
[123] Bonwick, *Western Victoria, Its Geography, Geology, and Social Condition*, p.159.
[124] Bonwick, *Western Victoria, Its Geography, Geology, and Social Condition*, pp.175-176.
[125] *Border Watch*, 28 October 1865, p.3.
[126] *Adelaide Observer*, 14 June 1856, p.3.
[127] *Hamilton Spectator*, 20 December 1910, p.6.
[128] *South Australian Register*, 7 June 1856, p.3.
[129] *South Australian Register*, 23 August 1856, p.3.
[130] *South Australian Register*, Friday 6 June 1856, p.2 & *Adelaide Observer*, 5 July 1856, p.5.
[131] *The Cornwall Chronicle,* 18 June 1856, p.2.
[132] *The Shipping Gazette and Sydney General Trade List*, 1 September 1856, p.191.
[133] *Adelaide Times*, 18 October 1856, p.3.
[134] Despatch from Governor Sir R. G. MacDonnell, October 15, 1857 in *Adelaide Observer*, 5 June 1858, p.7.
[135] Despatch from Governor Sir R. G. MacDonnell, October 15, 1857 in *Adelaide Observer*, 5 June 1858, p.7.
[136] *Adelaide Times*, 18 October 1856, p.3.
[137] *Adelaide Times*, 18 October 1856, p.3.
[138] *The Maitland Mercury and Hunter River General Advertiser*, 10 July 1856, p.3.
[139] *Bendigo Advertiser*, 23 July 1856, p.3.
[140] *The Age*, 14 October 1856, p.7.
[141] *Argus*, 1 August 1856, p.4.
[142] *Adelaide Times*, 23 January 1857, p.1.
[143] *Mount Alexander Mail*, 13 August 1858, p.6.
[144] *The Cornwall Chronicle*, 17 December 1856, p.5, 14 January 1857, p.5 & *Launceston Examiner*, 6 December 1856, p.3. See *Argus*, 27 June 1854, p.5.
[145] *South Australian Register*, 18 March 1857, p.2.
[146] *South Australian Register*, 26 January 1857, p.2.
[147] *South Australian Register*, 5 January 1858, p.2.

[148] *Bendigo Advertiser*, 28 September 1857, p.2, *South Australian Register*, 5 January 1858, p.2.
[149] *Adelaide Observer*, 7 February 1857, p.8.
[150] *Adelaide Observer*, 21 March 1857, p.1.
[151] *Adelaide Times*, 1 April 1857, p.2.
[152] *Bendigo Advertiser*, 20 May 1857, p.2.
[153] *South Australian Register*, 3 June 1857, p.3.
[154] *South Australian Register*, 5 January 1858, p.2.
[155] Despatch from Governor Sir R. G. MacDonnell, October 15, 1857 in *Adelaide Observer*, 5 June 1858, p.7.
[156] *South Australian Register*, 9 June 1857, p.2.
[157] *Adelaide Observer*, 2 May 1857, p.5.
[158] *South Australian Register*, 9 April 1857, p.3.
[159] *South Australian Register*, 9 April 1857, p.3.
[160] *South Australian Register*, 9 April 1857, p.3.

Chapter 5

[161] *South Australian Register*, 10 March 1856, p.2.
[162] *The Argus*, 2 June 1855, p.4.
[163] *South Australian Register*, 7 June 1856, p.3.
[164] *Bendigo Advertiser*, 20 May 1857, p.2.
[165] *Adelaide Times*, 12 March 1856, p.2.
[166] *Sydney Morning Herald*, 19 December 1856, p.4.
[167] *Argus*, 31 December 1857, p.5 & 24 December 1857, p.5.
[168] *The Age*, 21 January 1859, p.6.
[169] *Mount Alexander Mail*, 13 August 1858, p.6.
[170] *Mount Alexander Mail*, 13 August 1858, p.6.
[171] *Mount Alexander Mail*, 13 August 1858, p.6.
[172] *South Australian Advertiser*, 26 August 1861, p.5.
[173] *Mount Alexander Mail*, 22 April 1863, p.3.
[174] *The Herald*, 5 September 1862, p.6.
[175] *Hamilton Spectator and Grange District Advertiser*, 12 September 1862, p.4.
[176] *Portland Guardian and Normanby General Advertiser*, 23 April 1863, p.3.
[177] *Portland Guardian and Normanby General Advertiser*, 23 April 1863, p.3.
[178] *Portland Guardian and Normanby General Advertiser*, 23 April 1863, p.3.
[179] *Hamilton Spectator and Grange District Advertiser*, 10 April 1863, p.3.

[180] *Hamilton Spectator and Grange District Advertiser*, 17 April 1863, p.3.
[181] *Border Watch*, 7 August 1863, p.2.
[182] *The Star*, 12 August 1863, p.2.
[183] *Hamilton Spectator and Grange District Advertiser*, 21 August 1863, p.2.
[184] *Leader*, 5 September 1863, p.2.
[185] *South Australian Register*, 14 August 1863, p.3.
[186] *The Argus*, 8 September 1863, p.4.

Chapter 6

[187] *South Australian Register*, 8 April 1856, p.3.
[188] For examples, *The Age*, 31 March 1856, p.2 & *The Argus*, 1 August 1856, p.4.
[189] See for example *Williams's Melbourne almanac 1858*, p.27.
[190] *The Argus*, 1 August 1856, p.4.
[191] *The Argus*, 1 August 1856, p.5.
[192] Despatch No. 198, to Secretary of State for Colonies, Government House, Adelaide, 26 November 1857.
[193] *Adelaide Times*, 17 April 1857, p.2.
[194] *South Australian Register*, 5 February 1856, p.2.
[195] *Adelaide Times*, 31 May 1856, p.2.
[196] *Adelaide Times*, 5 June 1856, p.2.
[197] *Adelaide Times*, 20 February 1856, p.2.
[198] *Adelaide Times*, 7 July 1856, p.2.
[199] *The Cornwall Chronicle*, 12 July 1856, p.5.
[200] *Portland Guardian and Normanby General Advertiser*, 27 August 1856, p.2.
[201] Private journal of J. R. Ewens, 16 June 1856.
[202] *Adelaide Observer*, 5 July 1856, p.4.
[203] *Adelaide Observer*, 18 April 1857, p.4.
[204] *The Star*, 12 June 1857, p.3.
[205] Despatch from Governor Sir R. G. MacDonnell, October 15, 1857 in *Adelaide Observer*, 5 June 1858, p.7.
[206] Melville, Henry Dudley, 'Compensation for A Life's Service under Civil Service Regulations of South Australia 1887', Volume 2, 1887, p.112.
[207] Guichen Bay Police, 14 August 1857.
[208] *South Australian Register*, 12 September 1857, p.4.
[209] See p.47 above.
[210] *South Australian Weekly Chronicle*, 16 August 1862, p.2.
[211] *South Australian Register*, 14 August 1863, p.3.

[212] *Adelaide Times*, 24 March 1857, p.3.
[213] *The Argus*, 19 February 1857, p.6.
[214] *South Australian Register*, 8 April 1856, p.3.
[215] *The Star*, 29 July 1856, p.2.
[216] *South Australian Register*, 17 June 1856, p.3.
[217] *South Australian Register,* 5 February 1856, p.2.
[218] *Adelaide Times*, 3 June 1856, p.3.
[219] Chandler, J. *Forty Years in the Wilderness*, E. Wyatt, Printer, 1893, p.75.
[220] *Weekly Times*, 16 October 1920, p.29.
[221] *The Argus*, 4 May 1857, p.6.
[222] *The Star*, 20 April 1857, p.3.
[223] *Adelaide Times*, 26 January 1857, p.2.
[224] *The Age*, 12 September 1862, p.5.
[225] *South Australian Register*, 8 April 1863, p.3.

Chapter 7

[226] *Adelaide Observer*, 12 April 1856, p.3.
[227] *Adelaide Observer*, 14 June 1856, p.3.
[228] *Adelaide Observer*, 14 June 1856, p.3.
[229] Chandler, J., *Forty Years in the Wilderness*, E. Wyatt, Printer, 1893, p.70.
[230] *Adelaide Times*, 3 June 1856, p.3.
[231] *Portland Guardian*, 26 June 1857, p.2.
[232] *Geelong Advertiser*, 4 September 1862, p.2.
[233] *Adelaide Times*, 3 June 1856, p.3.
[234] Woods, Ten Years in the Bush, p.263.
[235] Bonwick, *Western Victoria, Its Geography, Geology, and Social Condition*, p.131.
[236] Woods, Ten Years in the Bush, p.264.
[237] Woods, Ten Years in the Bush, p,264.
[238] *The Age*, 10 April 1855, p.5.
[239] For example, Rolls, Eric, *Sojourners: Flowers and the Wide Sea*, University of Queensland Press, 1992, p.147.
[240] *South Australian Register*, 13 April 1852, p.3.
[241] *South Australian Register*, 16 March 1852, p.3.
[242] *Adelaide Times*, 24 March 1857, p.3. *Bathurst Free Press and Mining Journal*, 30 July 1856, p.2.
[243] *Adelaide Observer*, 7 February 1857, p.8.
[244] *South Australian Register*, 1 April 1857, p.2.
[245] *The Moreton Bay Courier*, 2 May 1857, p.3, reproducing from the *Melbourne Herald*.

[246] *Adelaide Observer*, 6 June 1857, p.2.
[247] *The Argus*, 19 February 1857, p.6.
[248] Woods, Ten Years in the Bush, p.264.
[249] *South Australian Register*, 3 June 1857, p.3.
[250] *Register*, 5 October 1908, p.7.

Chapter 8

[251] *Adelaide Observer*, 30 December 1843, p.4.
[252] *South Australian Record and Australasian Chronicle*, 22 February 1840, p.7 and in 1852, Ragless, *Oliver's diary*, p.17.
[253] Despatch from Governor Sir R. G. MacDonnell, October 15, 1857 in *Adelaide Observer*, 5 June 1858, p.7.
[254] *South Australian Register*, 17 February 1864, p.3.
[255] Graham Jenkin, *Conquest of the Ngarrindjeri*, Adelaide: Rigby, 1979, p.11.
[256] Penny Rudduck, *European Heritage of the Coorong: A general survey of the sites of Early European Heritage of the area now comprising the Coorong National Park and Coorong Game Reserve*, National Parks and Wildlife Service. May, 1982, pp.14-16.
[257] Kungari Aboriginal Cultural Association.
[258] Bonwick, *Western Victoria, Its Geography, Geology, and Social Condition*, p.178.
[259] Bonwick, *Western Victoria, Its Geography, Geology, and Social Condition*, p.159.
[260] *The Maitland Mercury and Hunter River General Advertiser*, 30 November 1844, p.4. See also Colonial Frontier Massacres in Australia, 1788-1930, https://c21ch.newcastle.edu.au/colonialmassacres/map.php
[261] Bonwick, *Western Victoria, Its Geography, Geology, and Social Condition*, p.159.
[262] Paul Memmott, *Gunyah, Goondie and Wurley: The Aboriginal architecture of Australia*, St Lucia, University of Queensland Press, 2007, pp.193-196.
[263] Woods, Ten Years in the Bush, pp.264-265.
[264] *South Australian Register*, 13 April 1852, p.3.
[265] *Weekly Times*, 16 October 1920, p.29.

Chapter 9

[266] *Adelaide Times*, 5 March 1856, p.3. [Other reports on loads carried by bamboo poles]

[267] *South Australian Register*, 28 August 1857, p.2 & 9 April 1857, p.3. Challenge - *Sydney Morning Herald*, 14 July 1857, p.3, Young America - *Adelaide Observer*, 18 April 1857, p.4.
[268] *Adelaide Observer*, 14 June 1856, p.5.
[269] *South Australian Register*, 9 June 1856, p.2.
[270] *South Australian Register*, 28 August 1857, p.2.
[271] *Adelaide Observer*, 7 February 1857, p.8.
[272] *Adelaide Observer*, 5 July 1856, p.1 & *South Australian Register*, 22 August 1856, p.3.
[273] Guichen Bay Police, 1 February 1857.
[274] *South Australian Register*, 27 May 1857, p.2.
[275] *The Argus*, 19 February 1857, p.6.
[276] *The Register*, 22 January 1915, p.4.
[277] *South Australian Register*, 28 August 1857, p.2, 4 September 1857, p.3 & *Launceston Examiner*, 1 September 1857, p.2.
[278] *Adelaide Times*, 8 July 1857, p.2.
[279] *Adelaide Observer*, 16 August 1856, p.7.
[280] *Portland Guardian and Normanby General Advertiser*, 29 July 1857, p.2.
[281] *Portland Guardian and Normanby General Advertiser*, 13 April 1857, p.3.
[282] Admission papers, Colonial Lunatic Asylum, 1858 unnumbered, John Chinaman, State Records SA: GRS 13461/00001 & *Adelaide Observer*, 24 July 1858, p.4.
[283] *South Australian Register*, 1 July 1856, p.2.
[284] *Adelaide Observer*, 12 July 1856, p.3.
[285] *South Australian Register*, 15 August 1856, p.2.
[286] *Adelaide Observer*, 16 August 1856, p.7.
[287] *Weekly Times*, 16 October 1920, p.29.
[288] *The Argus*, 25 July 1856, p.6.
[289] *The Star*, 20 July 1857, p.3.
[290] *The Argus*, 7 September 1857, p.6.
[291] *The Star*, 12 October 1857, p.3. In Adelaide, *South Australian Register*, 15 August 1856, p.2.
[292] *The Star*, 14 August 1857, p.3.
[293] *The Star*, 30 October 1857, p.3.
[294] *The Star*, 14 January 1858, p.2.
[295] Ah Poo, *The Star*, 12 October 1857, p.3; Chow Nung, *The Star*, 23 November 1857, p.3; Ah Tin, *The Star*, 27 September 1858, p.3.
[296] *The Star*, 30 October 1857, p.3.
[297] *The Age*, 21 January 1859, p.6.
[298] *Border Watch*, 12 September 1862, p.4.
[299] *Geelong Advertiser*, 4 September 1862, p.2.

[300] *The Star*, 4 September 1863, p.2.
[301] *Adelaide Times*, 24 March 1857, p.3 and *Adelaide Observer*, 23 August 1862, p.4.
[302] *The Age*, 6 October 1857, p.6.
[303] *Adelaide Observer*, 23 August 1862, p.4.
[304] *Bendigo Advertiser*, 6 September 1862, p.3.
[305] *Adelaide Observer*, 31 July 1858, p.4.
[306] *South Australian Register*, 15 July 1857, p.3.
[307] *Adelaide Times*, 27 March 1857, p.2.
[308] *South Australian Register*, 4 April 1857, p.3.
[309] *South Australian Register*, 9 April 1857, p.3 & *Adelaide Times*, 9 April 1857, p.2.
[310] *South Australian Weekly Chronicle*, 16 August 1862, p.2.
[311] *South Australian Weekly Chronicle*, 16 August 1862, p.2.
[312] *The Star*, 10 March 1857, p.2.
[313] *The Argus*, 7 August 1857, p.6.
[314] *South Australian Register*, 24 March 1857, p.3.
[315] Foster, *Letter book,* September 1855 to December 1859.
[316] *The Age*, 5 June 1857, p.5.
[317] *Ovens and Murray Advertiser*, 4 September 1857, p.3.
[318] See, https://monumentaustralia.org.au/themes/landscape/settlement/display/30069-canton-lead
[319] *The Age*, 1 June 1857, p.3.
[320] *Freeman's Journal*, 20 June 1857, p.2 & *Ovens and Murray Advertiser*, 25 June 1857, p.2.
[321] *The Star*, 21 July 1857, p.2 for a series of courts cases and convictions.
[322] *The Star*, 20 August 1857, p.2.
[323] *The Age*, 11 February 1858, p.5.

Chapter 10

[324] Sprengel, *Robe's Chinese invasion*, pp.6-7.
[325] Cawthorne, *The Long Journey*, p.2.
[326] Horsfall, *March to Big Gold Mountain*, p.3.
[327] *Adelaide Times*, 26 January 1856, p.4.
[328] *Adelaide Observer*, 6 June 1857, p.2.
[329] Rolls, *Sojourners*, p.135.
[330] *Adelaide Times*, 26 January 1856, p.4 in a report dated September 1855.

[331] Henry Dudley Melville, 'Compensation for A Life's Service under Civil Service Regulations of South Australia 1887', Volume 2, 1887, pp.111-112.
[332] Such as Rolls, *Sojourners*, p.135. Sprengel, *Robe's Chinese invasion*, p.19.
[333] State Records SA: GRG5/159, Guichen Bay Police Station Records 1851 – 1863 and State Library of South Australia, D 8334 (L), Private journal of J. R. Ewens, Police trooper, 1853-1862.
[334] Guichen Bay Police, 19 January 1857.
[335] Private journal of J. R. Ewens, 20 & 21 June 1856.
[336] Guichen Bay Police, 1 February 1857, *Phaeton*; 27 April 1857, *Sultana*; 26 June 1857, *Koenig William II* (referred to as *King William the Second* and *Koning Willem De Tweede* by the police).
[337] Guichen Bay Police, 18 March 1857, *William Miles*.]
[338] Guichen Bay Police, 21 March 1857. For a similar case a few years later of a 'dead body of a young man' see *South Australian Register*, 24 October 1860, p.3.
[339] Guichen Bay Police, 21 May 1857, *Pudsey Dawson*.
[340] Guichen Bay Police, 14 August 1857, *Salsette* (written as *Sanlsette* by police).
[341] Woods, Ten Years in the Bush, p.263. For an account of an 'interesting and amusing' Woods lecture see, *The Mercury*, 18 August 1875, p.3.
[342] *South Australian Register*, 1 April 1857, p.2.
[343] Guichen Bay Police, 18-19 March 1857, *William Miles*.
[344] Guichen Bay Police, 21 & 22 March 1857.
[345] Guichen Bay Police, 23 May 1857.
[346] Guichen Bay Police, 24 May 1857. Destitute Board, *Adelaide Times*, 16 June 1857, p.2.
[347] Rolls, *Sojourners*, p.135.
[348] Rolls, *Sojourners*, p.136 & Cawthorne, p.5, Sprengel, p.12. John Brewer, 1838-1914, Reminiscences of John Brewer (Notes written in 1968 by John L. Cantrill/Cantrell), State Library of South Australia, D Piece (Archival), D 7378(L), p.7.
[349] *South Australian Register*, 31 March 1856, p.3.
[350] *The Argus*, 8 October 1857, p.5.
[351] Woods, Ten Years in the Bush, p.265.
[352] Foster, *Letter book*, September 1855 to December 1859.
[353] Foster, *Letter book*, October 18th 1857, p.682 & October 24th 1857, p.684.
[354] *Hamilton Spectator and Grange District Advertiser*, 20 November 1863, p.2.
[355] Woods, Ten Years in the Bush, p.265.

[356] *Weekly Times*, 16 October 1920, p.29.
[357] *Weekly Times*, 16 October 1920, p.29.
[358] Bonwick, *Western Victoria, Its Geography, Geology, and Social Condition*, p.131.
[359] *Border Watch*, 20 July 1867, p.2.
[360] *The Star*, 29 July 1856, p.2.
[361] *The Star*, 20 August 1857, p.2.
[362] *Weekly Times*, 16 October 1920, p.29.
[363] *Geelong Advertiser*, 4 September 1862, p.2.
[364] Ritchie, *Guichen Bay to Canton*, repeats most of these myths.
[365] *South Australian Register*, 3 July 1841, pp.2-3.
[366] Thomas Burr and G. Grey, "Account of Governor G. Grey's Exploratory Journey along the South-Eastern Sea-Board of South Australia." *The Journal of the Royal Geographical Society of London* 15 (1845), p.165.
[367] Burr and Grey, "Account of Governor G. Grey's Exploratory Journey", p.171.
[368] Burr and Grey, "Account of Governor G. Grey's Exploratory Journey", p.173.
[369] *South Australian Register*, 16 March 1852, p.3.
[370] *South Australian Register*, 3 July 1841, p.3, on the Coorong 'the native wells are numerous'; *Adelaide Observer*, 3 April 1852, p.2, 'wells established on the-overland line to Mount Alexander'; *South Australian Register*, 16 March 1852, p.3, 'survey party ... were sinking a well'; Blake, L. J. *Gold Escort*, Hawthorn Press, 1971, pp.31-34, 'by establishing definite water points, had made the route available for all overland travellers', p.34, quoting Maclaren's survey in 1852; and in early 1852, 'the native well' and 'another well', Ragless, *Oliver's diary*, p.17.
[371] *South Australian Register*, 3 July 1841, pp.2-3.
[372] Penny Rudduck, *European Heritage of the Coorong: A general survey of the sites of Early European Heritage of the area now comprising the Coorong National Park and Coorong Game Reserve*, National Parks and Wildlife Service. May, 1982, p.31.
[373] *South Australian Register*, 11 June 1856, p.4.
[374] Moloney, David, Rowe, David, Jellie, Pamela, "Former Robinson Water Tank, The Bullock Track", *Shire of Melton Heritage Study, Volume 5*, 2006, np.
[375] Roger Luebbers, *The Archaeology of Chinamans Wells and Hacks Station, The Coorong, South Australia*, report to Department of Environment & Natural Resources, Adelaide, 1995, p.37.
[376] *Adelaide Observer*, 25 October 1856, p.7.
[377] Private journal of J. R. Ewens, 6 April 1857.

[378] Luebbers, *The archaeology of Chinamans Wells*, p.iv.
[379] Luebbers, *The archaeology of Chinamans Wells*, p.38.
[380] Luebbers, *The archaeology of Chinamans Wells*, p.43.
[381] Luebbers, *The archaeology of Chinamans Wells*, p.43.
[382] Horsfall, *March to Big Gold Mountain*, 28 and Alexander Barrowman, *Old days and old ways*, Robe, S. Aust., A. H. Barrowman, 1971, p.40.
[383] Luebbers, *The archaeology of Chinamans Wells*, p.44.
[384] Z. Stanin, "From Li Chun to Yong Kit: a market garden on the Loddon, 1851-1912", Paper in special issue: Active Voices, Hidden Histories: The Chinese in Colonial Australia, *Journal of Australian Colonial History*, 6 (2004), p.30, including references by others of 'square' wells.
[385] Luebbers, *The archaeology of Chinamans Wells*, p.18.
[386] Ragless, *Oliver's diary*, p.18.
[387] *Adelaide Observer*, 3 April 1852, p.2 and Blake, *Gold Escort*, p.33.
[388] *Border Watch*, 18 October 1876, p.3.
[389] *Border Watch*, 12 July 1876, p.3.
[390] Luebbers, *The archaeology of Chinamans Wells*, p.13.
[391] Luebbers, *The archaeology of Chinamans Wells*, p.14.
[392] *The Mail*, 2 December 1933, p.1.
[393] Lindsay, H.A., "Who Did Build the Chinaman's Well?", *Sunday Mail*, 23 October 1965, p.44; "Mystery of Well", *Sunday Mail*, 30 October 1965, np and "In a well, the wisdom of the East", *Walkabout*, 6 April 1966, np.
[394] Gordon Copland, *Event driven transitory migration the case of the Chinese migration through South Australia between 1854 and 1864*, Honours Thesis, Finders University, 1998, p.78.
[395] Snoek, W., *Archaeological report of Chinamans Wells, the Coorong National Park*, South Australian Department of Environment and Planning, 1984, pp.1-4.
[396] Snoek, *Archaeological report of Chinamans Wells*, p.1.
[397] Snoek, *Archaeological report of Chinamans Wells*, p.7.
[398] Snoek, *Archaeological report of Chinamans Wells*, p.2 & Luebbers, *The archaeology of Chinamans Wells*, p.10. For example, *Southern Argus*, 8 February 1868, p.2.
[399] *Adelaide Observer*, 30 January 1864, p.1. *The Advertiser*, 7 August 1941, p.9.
[400] Luebbers, *The archaeology of Chinamans Wells*, p.v.
[401] *Adelaide Observer*, 6 August 1864, p.6.
[402] *Adelaide Observer*, 2 July 1864, p.3.
[403] *South Australian Register*, 28 January 1867, p.1.
[404] *South Australian Register*, 15 March 1864, p.1.

[405] Luebbers, *The archaeology of Chinamans Wells*, p.13.
[406] Luebbers, *The archaeology of Chinamans Wells*, p.16.
[407] Luebbers, *The archaeology of Chinamans Wells*, p.16.
[408] Luebbers, *The archaeology of Chinamans Wells*, p.17.
[409] Luebbers, *The archaeology of Chinamans Wells*, p.25.
[410] Robert Edwards, "Chinese coins from an Aboriginal camp-site on the Coorong, South Australia", *Australian Numismatic Journal*, Vol.17, No.3, July-September 1966, pp.102-105.
[411] Luebbers, *The archaeology of Chinamans Wells*, p.25.
[412] Luebbers, *The archaeology of Chinamans Wells*, p.25.
[413] See, https://www.walkingsa.org.au/walk/find-a-place-to-walk/chinamans-well-historic-site-journey-to-gold-walk-coorong-national-park/
[414] National Parks South Australia, *Coorong National Park, Coorong Self-guided History Trail*, 6. Chinaman's Well, 2020?
[415] See above p.99 for Lindsay.
[416] Penny Paton, "Chinamans Well" in Paton, D. C. *At the end of the river: the Coorong and lower lakes*, ATF Press, Hindmarsh, SA, 2010, pp.40-41.
[417] Ragless, *Oliver's diary*, p.18.
[418] Rolls, *Sojourners*, p.137.
[419] *Hamilton Spectator and Grange District Advertiser*, 10 June 1864, p.2.
[420] For the story of the Aboriginal cricket team see, "Johnny Mullagh & First XI", Harrow Discovery Centre, https://harrow.org.au/history/johnny-mullagh-first-xi/
[421] *Bell's Life in Victoria and Sporting Chronicle*, 25 August 1866, p.2.
[422] Timothy Hubbard, *Mount Sturgeon's 'Chinese' Wall: A Planning Report on its Significance*, Heritage Matters, Port Fairy, Victoria, 2018.
[423] Bruce Munday, *Those dry-stone walls: stories from South Australia's stone age*, Wakefield Press, 2012, p.33.
[424] *Dry Stone Walls*, Great Ocean Road Regional Tourism, 2023, https://volcaniclakesandplains.com.au/explore/dry-stone-walls/
[425] McAlpine, R. A., *The Shire of Hampden, 1863-1963*, Hampden Shire Council, 1963, p.103.
[426] Munday, *Those dry-stone walls*, p.33.
[427] *Adelaide Observer*, 10 October 1857, p.1.
[428] *The Hobart Town Advertiser*, 20 August 1858, p.3.
[429] *Hamilton Spectator and Grange District Advertiser*, 25 April 1862, p.3.
[430] Ritchie, *Guichen Bay to Canton*, p.35.

[431] See also, Dunkeld and District Historical Museum, Transcribing and Editing of audio tape of Monthly meeting held on 5th November, 1990 – The Chinese Invasion.
[432] *Bendigo Advertiser*, 20 May 1857, p.2.
[433] *South Australian Register*, 16 March 1852, p.3.
[434] *South Australian Register*, 16 March 1852, p.3.
[435] Ritchie, *Guichen Bay to Canton*, p.35.
[436] *The Star*, 12 August 1858, p.3 & *The Age*, 28 September 1858, p.6.
[437] *The Age*, 28 September 1858, p.6.
[438] *Bendigo Advertiser*, 6 September 1862, p.3 and *Portland Guardian and Normanby General Advertiser*, 23 April 1863, p.3.
[439] Golden Dragon Museum, *The Walk from Robe*, p.15.
[440] *Adelaide Observer*, 2 October 1858, p.3.
[441] *Adelaide Observer*, 31 October 1863, p.1.
[442] *Hamilton Spectator and Grange District Advertiser*, 27 May 1864, p.3.
[443] *Portland Guardian and Normanby General Advertiser*, 14 January 1867, p.2.
[444] *Border Watch*, 21 November 1868, p.3.
[445] See Victorian CEDT Index, https://www.cafhov.com/vic-cedt-index
[446] *Hamilton Spectator*, 28 February 1874, p.4.
[447] *Hamilton Spectator*, 26 August 1874, p.4.
[448] *Hamilton Spectator*, 13 February 1875, p.4.
[449] *Hamilton Spectator*, 29 January 1876, p.4.
[450] *Hamilton Spectator*, 26 January 1876, p.2.
[451] *Border Watch*, 17 October, 1877, p.3 and 25 May 1878, p.2.
[452] *Hamilton Spectator*, 17 February 1880, p.3.
[453] *Hamilton Spectator*, 29 January 1880, p.2.
[454] *The Horsham Times*, 13 July 1883, p.3.
[455] *Hamilton Spectator*, 20 February 1877, p.4.
[456] *The Horsham Times*, 24 November 1885, p.2.
[457] *The Horsham Times*, 17 April, 1883, p.3.
[458] *The Horsham Times*, 7 April, 1887, p.2.
[459] *Hamilton Spectator*, 22 September 1885, p.3 & *The Argus*, 2 May 1885, p.4.
[460] *Weekly Times*, 20 March 1886, p..3.
[461] *Hamilton Spectator*, 8 November 1887, p.4.
[462] *Hamilton Spectator*, 5 February 1885, p.3.
[463] *The Horsham Times*, 19 July 1889, p.2.
[464] *The Narracoorte Herald*, 26 April 1895, p.3.
[465] *The Age*, 24 July 1906, p.6.
[466] *The Horsham Times*, 23 October 1906, p.4.

[467] See Barry McGowan, Reconsidering race: The Chinese experience on the goldfields of southern New South Wales, *Australian Historical Studies*, October 2004, Vol.36 (124), p.312-331.

Chapter 11

[468] *Hamilton Spectator*, 20 December 1910, p.6.
[469] Dunkeld and District Historical Museum, Transcribing and Editing of audio tape of Monthly meeting held on 5th November, 1990 – The Chinese Invasion, pp.3-5.
[470] Ian MacKinnon, 4/11/1990, 'Some brief comments', insert to Dunkeld and District Historical Museum, Transcribing and Editing of audio tape of Monthly meeting held on 5th November, 1990 – The Chinese Invasion.
[471] Ian MacKinnon, 4/11/1990, 'Some brief comments.'
[472] *Hamilton Spectator*?, June 1961. (From a clipping, Hamilton Historical Society, no day or page number.)
[473] 'Chinese at Coleraine', Coleraine Historical Society file document, 2017.
[474] 'Chinese at Coleraine', Coleraine Historical Society file document, 2017.
[475] Bonwick, *Western Victoria, Its Geography, Geology, and Social Condition*, p.157.
[476] *The Argus*, 27 March 1856, p.5.
[477] *Portland Guardian and Normanby General Advertiser*, 12 August 1861, p.2.
[478] *Hamilton Spectator and Grange District Advertiser*, 12 October 1861, p.2.
[479] *The Ballarat Star*, 3 October 1865, p.1.
[480] *Portland Guardian*, 14 October 1901, p.3.
[481] *Coleraine Albion and Western Advertiser*, 24 December 1918, p.2.
[482] Smeaton, Thomas Dury, *Our Invasion by Chinese, 1865*, State Library of South Australia Research Notes RN 830. Cawthorne writing in 1974 and Sprengel in 1986, both possibly following Smeaton, also seem completely unaware of any arrivals by Chinese walkers before the *Land o' Cakes*, both describing it as a 'surprise' to Robe, Cawthorne, *The Long Journey*, p.1, Sprengel, *Robe's Chinese invasion*, p.6, and Horsfall follows this, Horsfall, *March to Big Gold Mountain*, p.4, as does the Golden Dragon Museum, *The Walk from Robe*, p.13.
[483] *Adelaide Observer*, 7 February 1857, p.8.
[484] Thomas Dury Smeaton, *Our Invasion by Chinese, 1865*, State Library of South Australia Research Notes RN 830.

[485] *The South Eastern Times*, 11 May 1928, p.3.
[486] Joseph Cooke Verco, Records, 1851 - 1924, State Library of South Australia, PRG 322/6.
[487] Roland Campbell, letter to Mr Smith, Kingston, 18 May 1941, Millicent, State Library of South Australia, PRG 497.
[488] Rolls, *Sojourners*, p.136.
[489] Luebbers, *The archaeology of Chinamans Wells*, p.16.
[490] Luebbers, *The archaeology of Chinamans Wells*, p.44.
[491] Hubbard, *Mount Sturgeon's 'Chinese' Wall*.
[492] J. Chandler, *Forty Years in the Wilderness*, E. Wyatt, Printer, 1893, p.84.
[493] Chandler, *Forty Years in the Wilderness*, p.75.
[494] *Border Watch*, 21 November 1868, p.3.
[495] *Adelaide Times*, 24 March 1857, p.3.
[496] For a discussion see, Karen Schamberger, "The Lambing Flat Riots And Its Legacies 1861-2021", Young Historical Museum, July 2021, https://younghistoricalmuseum.wordpress.com/2021/07/15/the-lambing-flat-riots-and-its-legacies-1861-2021/
[497] *Quiz and the Lantern*, 26 August 1897, p.4.
[498] For example, *The Register*, 26 July 1901, p.5; 15 December 1904, p.3 & *The Advertiser*, 8 October 1906, p.6.
[499] *The Mail*, 6 June 1925, p.17.
[500] *The Register*, 3 March 1928, p.5.
[501] *The Register*, 14 May 1928, p.13.
[502] *The Adelaide Chronicle*, 12 March 1936, p.16. A similar account was published a few years before in *The Adelaide Chronicle*, 31 August 1933, p.14 and again a decade later in *The Adelaide Chronicle*, 21 November 1946, p.12.
[503] *The Adelaide Chronicle*, 12 March 1936, p.16.
[504] See, bones, *The Adelaide Chronicle*, 5 May 1932, p.39; overboard, *Burra Record*, 4 February 1936, p.4; well, *The Advertiser*, 1 September 1936, p.51; guides, *The Mail*, 21 July 1945, p.5.
[505] *News*, 1 June 1939, p.17 and *Narracoorte Herald*, 27 March 1942, p.4.
[506] *Border Watch*, 7 August 1945, p.2 and *The Advertiser*, 20 November 1946, p.10.
[507] *The Adelaide Chronicle*, 21 November 1946, p.12.
[508] *The South Eastern Times*, 29 November 1946, p.2 & 6 December 1946, p.4.
[509] Luebbers, *The archaeology of Chinamans Wells*, p.69.
[510] Luebbers, *The archaeology of Chinamans Wells*, p.69.
[511] Penny Rudduck, *European Heritage of the Coorong: A general survey of the sites of Early European Heritage of the area now*

comprising the Coorong National Park and Coorong Game Reserve, National Parks and Wildlife Service, May, 1982, p.39.

[512] Robe Customs House Museum information panels, 'The Chinese' & 'Walk to the Diggings'.

[513] Rolls, *Sojourners*, p.138.

[514] The Treks from Robe by Cash Brown, https://victoriancollections.net.au/media/exhibitions/5fbd874fd5fa81 08043fc293//5fc8d9e89992142684f04d6a/original.pdf

[515] *Victor Harbour Times*, 20 September 1985, p.3.

[516] Louise Edwards, "Victims, Apologies, and the Chinese in Australia", *Journal of Chinese Overseas*, *15* (1), pp.62-88, 2019.

[517] Schamberger, "The Lambing Flat Riots and Its Legacies 1861-2021".

[518] See Ghassan Hage, *White Nation: Fantasies of White Supremacy in a Multicultural Society*, Routledge, 2000 for a discussion of the limits of multiculturalism.

[519] For an explanation of this trope see, John Fitzgerald, "China's 'Century of Humiliation' and Chinese-Australian History", *Chinese Southern Diaspora Studies*, Volume Eight, 2019, pp.230-235.

Index

Aboriginal, 123, 126, 185, 216
(Bungandidj (Wattatonga), Djab Wurrung, Gunditjmara
(Koroite), Jardiwadjali, Ngarrindjeri, Tanganekald)
see also, indigenous, natives

Adelaide, *passim*
see also, Port Adelaide

Amoy (aka Xiamen), 17, 18, 215, 222, 261
see also coolies, indentured labourers

Ararat, 7, 25, 89, 91, 93, 123, 149, 151, 214, 222, 249
see also, Canton Lead

archaeological/archaeologists, 196-198, 201, 246, 260

arrest(s), 86, 93, 167, 179, 218, 220
see also, fines

Australian colonies, 4, 8, 13, 22, 34, 38, 56, 57, 56
see also, colonies

British, 5, 12, 14, 20, 21, 22, 33-35, 43, 55, 57, 91, 122, 123, 147, 207, 226, 265

California, 4, 15, 33-35, 43, 60

Canton (aka Guangdong), 18, 25, 30, 33-35, 151, 251, 252

Canton Lead, 25, 152
see also, Ararat

Cantonese, 14, 15, 18, 261, 264
see also, dialect

celestials, 9, 21, 67, 76, 89, 90, 112, 140, 174, 175, 202, 219, 226, 233, 244, 255
see also, Chinaman

charterparty/charterparties, 6, 55, 58, 83, 85, 147, 156, 157,

China (aka Qing Empire), 1,5, 12, 14,18-20, 27, 35, 38, 40, 53, 55, 66, 71, 83, 91, 120, 122, 139, 144, 156, 158, 170, 178, 191, 192, 195, 197, 201, 229, 264, 265
see also, Pearl River Delta, Qing Empire

Chinaman, 17, 32, 62, 76, 89, 94, 95, 105, 134, 136, 143, 165, 168, 174, 182, 256
see also, celestials, Chinamans Well

Chinamans Well, 181, 182, 186, 190, 193, 194, 196-207, 210, 211, 247, 256, 259, 260
see also, myths, oral tradition, stone walls, woolsheds

Chinese, *passim*
see also, celestials, Chinaman

Chinese individuals
    Achee, 17
    Ah Chin, 227
    Ah Chum, 227
    Ah Chung, 227
    Ah Me, 227
    Ah Pay, 227
    Ah Wan, 227
    Atong, 128, 129
    Ayun, 54-58, 64, 266
    Chang Lee, 227
    Ching Wot, 227
    Choong Ah Chee, 226
    Chu a Luk, 63, 64
    Chung Yet, 227
    Cossey, 17

Dummy, 230
Fong Ah Mun, 56
Ho A Low (aka Howloa), 56
Hong Sip, 228, 229
Jen-Song, 129
Lee Gee Kwong, 226
Lee Tew Hack, 226
Lee Young, 226
Meng Kim, 238, 239
Moy Hing, 225
Piggu, 17
Pon-Sa, 63
Sue Ah Toy, 226
Sun Kwong War, 227
Wah Chan, 227
Yung Hing, 128, 147

Chinese Protector, 36, 45, 77, 88, 149, 172, 173, 219, 250, 256

colonies, 13, 20, 21, 35, 36, 57, 122, 215
    see also, Australian colonies

convicts, 36, 212, 213

coolies, 28, 33
    see also, Amoy, indentured labourers

credit-ticket, 6, 20, 29, 40, 42, 217, 261
    see also, debt (indebted)

debt (indebted), 52, 149, 178, 179, 247
    see also, credit-ticket

dialect(s), 18-20, 22, 137, 251,

discrimination, 20, 35, 219, 264, 265, 269
    see also, racism

doctor(s), 60, 61, 128, 129, 141, 155, 226, 249

European, 4, 6, 14, 18, 27, 28, 34, 35, 37, 38, 40, 51, 57, 105, 108, 109, 110, 123, 125, 137, 140, 180, 181, 192, 209, 227, 229, 247, 260, 268
see also, white, White Australia policy, white guilt

fine(s), 60, 61, 63, 87, 89, 101, 103, 108, 168
see also, arrests

gold/goldfields, *passim*

Gold Escort, 7, 67, 262
see also, Tolmer, Capt.

Guichen Bay, *see* Robe (Robetown)

Hong Kong, 55, 128, 131, 146-148, 155, 157-160, 164, 231, 261, 266

indigenous, 20, 21, 22, 36, 37, 38, 122, 174, 210
see also Aboriginal, natives

immigration restriction, 21-22
see also, poll tax

indentured (labourers/workers), 17, 18, 215, 261

infrastructure, 14, 38, 155, 178, 207, 211, 215, 221, 222, 233
see also, Chinamans well, myths, stone walls, woolsheds

market gardens/gardeners, 155, 182, 192, 215, 221, 224-227, 231, 257

Melbourne (Port Phillip), 48-50, 54-56, 59-63, 77-79, 89, 96, 97, 100, 105, 115, 122, 131, 147, 158, 197

Melville, Henry (Sub-Collector of Customs, Robe), 81, 120, 162

merchants, 30, 31, 33, 35, 56, 57, 62, 64, 85, 147, 158, 177 migrant(s), 15, 259, 263-265, 267

Murray/Murray River, 10, 17, 23, 66-68, 74, 76, 77, 98, 132, 180

myth(s), (mythmaking, mythologised), 14, 154, 156, 169, 170, 178-180, 184, 196, 204, 208, 209, 211, 212, 214, 229, 231, 232-235, 238-240, 248, 249, 251-254, 258, 259, 261, 262, 266, 268, 269
see also, Chinamans Well, oral tradition, stone walls, woolsheds

natives, 17, 83, 122, 123
see also, Aborigines, indigenous

New South Wales (aka NSW), 2, 5, 8, 9, 12, 19, 23, 26, 33, 36, 38, 40, 76, 77, 218, 230, 259

Ngarrindjeri, 122, 123, 202, 260
see also, Aborigines, indigenous, natives

oral/oral tradition, 200, 201, 211, 222, 232, 234, 238, 240, 244-249, 262
see also, Chinamans Well, myths, stone walls, woolsheds

opium, 115, 121,

Opium War, 14, 34, 265

Pearl River Delta, 4, 6, 14, 16, 18-20, 22, 25, 28, 29, 33-35, 42-44, 49, 52, 95, 115, 127-28, 195, 248, 269, 281
see also China

poll tax, 6, 7, 9-11, 20, 32, 48, 57, 64, 88, 89, 93, 104, 106, 115, 120, 134, 153, 215, 218, 224, 228, 254, 261, 264, 266
see also, resident's tax, tonnage restriction

Port Adelaide, 2, 7, 9, 44, 45, 48, 49, 75, 79, 100, 160, 161, 217, 255

Qing Empire, 15, 16, 18, 34
see also China

Queensland, 23, 26, 33, 230, 231, 259

racism, 14, 22, 35, 153, 155, 259, 265, 269
see also, discrimination

resident's tax, 62, 64, 88, 93, 218
see also, poll tax, tonnage restriction

Robe (Guichen Bay, Robetown), *passim*

Robe Customs House Museum, 116, 117, 260

schooner(s), 49, 79, 100, 101, 164

> *Fame*, 101
> *Gem*, 100, 101
> *Skyrocket*, 49
> Vixen, 79
> > *see also*, ships, steamers

sheep, 14, 17, 91, 122, 124, 126, 174, 194, 216, 222, 248

ship(s), 79-83, 87, 93, 95, 101, 102, 104, 106, 113, 116, 128-132, 134, 144-147, 152, 154, 156-165, 167, 168, 173, 198, 208, 241, 261, 266

> *Alfred*, 77
> *Buonavista*, 104, 145
> *Challenge*, 128
> *Cornwall*, 100
> *Emma*, 30, 54, 55, 57, 58
> *Estrella do Norte*, 83, 98, 146, 147
> *Francis P. Sage*, 149
> *General Blanco*, 129
> *Investigator*, 81
> *Land o' Cakes*, 79, 80, 156, 158, 164, 241

Manhow, 129, 132
Mary Bradford, 92
Oracle, 81
Koenig William II
    (aka *King William Second*), 132, 146, 163, 164
Phaeton, 130, 131, 164
Pudsey Dawson, 168
Sultana, 164
William Miles, 81, 167
Young America, 128
    see also, schooners, steamers

Singapore, 17, 30, 49, 215

South Australia, *passim*

steamer(s), 7, 8, 10, 11, 48, 55, 68, 69, 74, 76-78, 81-83, 92, 95-98, 100, 101, 132, 156, 159, 160, 164, 169, 241

    Burra Burra, 48, 82, 97, 100, 132
    Havilah, 49, 92
    Jamestown, 74
    Juno, 8
    Launceston, 10, 44
    Leichhardt, 74
    Tamar, 78
    Vixen, 78
    White Swan, 7, 8, 97, 100, 132
    Wonga Wonga, 77, 97
    Young Australia, 55
    see also, schooners, ships

stone walls, 11, 125, 178, 207, 210, 211, 212-214, 220, 222, 223, 230, 233, 236, 247, 248, 258
    see also, Chinamans Well, myths, oral tradition, woolsheds

Sydney, 5, 7-9, 26, 60, 61, 77, 85, 89, 92, 94, 97

Tasmania (aka Van Diemen's Land), 5, 46, 76-79

Tolmer, Capt., 23, 24, 67, 70, 118, 180, 216, 262
   see also, Gold Escort

tonnage restriction, 5, 78, 87
   see also poll tax

Victoria(n), *passim*

villages, 6, 33, 35, 40, 43, 44, 49, 64, 95, 115, 125, 128, 142, 158, 161, 216, 231, 252
   see also, Pearl River Delta

White Australia policy, 155, 252-254, 256, 257, 262, 263
   see also European, white, white guilt

white, 4, 35, 37, 116, 126, 155, 177, 187, 188, 210, 224, 232, 252, 257-259, 262-264, 267, 268
   see also, European, White Australia policy, white guilt

white guilt, 263, 264, 267
   see also, European, white, White Australia policy

woolshed(s), 154, 178, 207-210, 212-214, 217, 220, 222. 230, 238, 252, 258, 280
   see also, Chinamans Well, oral tradition, myths, stone walls

www.ingramcontent.com/pod-product-compliance
Lightning Source LLC
LaVergne TN
LVHW051111080426
835510LV00018B/1990